Pasta
COOKBOOK

The Confident Cooking Promise of Success

Welcome to the world of Confident Cooking,
where recipes are double-tested by our team
of home economists to achieve a high standard
of success—and delicious results every time.

bay books

C O N T E

Green Olive and Eggplant Toss, page 27.

Minestrone with Pesto, page 32.

Gnocchi with Tomato Sauce, page 53.

Farfalle with Tuna, Mushrooms and Cream, page 73.

Semolina Gnocchi, page 110.

Baked Spaghetti Frittata, page 88.

The Publisher thanks the following for their assistance in the photography for this book:

Waterford Wedgewood;
Zyliss Australia;
Emile-Henry;
Antico's Fruitworld;
Nicholas;
Le Creuset.

Classic Lasagne, page 102.

The test kitchen where our recipes are double-tested by our team of home economists to achieve a high standard of success and delicious results every time.

When we test our recipes, we rate them for ease of preparation. The following cookery ratings are on the recipes in this book, making them easy to use and understand.

A single Cooking with Confidence symbol indicates a recipe that is simple and generally quick to make—perfect for beginners.

Two symbols indicate the need for just a little more care and a little more time.

Three symbols indicate special dishes that need more investment in time, care and patience—but the results are worth it.

IMPORTANT
Those who might be at risk from the effects of salmonella food poisoning (the elderly, pregnant women, young children and those suffering from immune deficiency diseases) should consult their doctor with any concerns about eating raw eggs.

Pasta and Cheese

Pasta can be as simple or as extravagant as you like—depending
upon its accompanying sauce. Most pasta dishes are enhanced
by the addition of cheese. Pasta, cheese and salad makes a
well-balanced and delicious meal.

HOW TO COOK PASTA

Use a very large pan of water. For
500 g (1 lb 2 oz) of pasta you will need
at least 4 litres (16 cups) of water.
Bring water, salted if desired, to a
rapid boil and add pasta gradually so
the water continues to boil. The pasta
should move freely to prevent it sticking together. Stir once with a long-
handled fork or spoon to prevent
pasta sticking to bottom of the pan.

Long pasta such as spaghetti
should be eased into the water rather
than broken. Hold one end and put
the other end in the boiling water. As
pasta softens, gently lower it into the
water until it is all immersed. Make
sure the water boils rapidly while
pasta is cooking. Do not cover pan.

Some people like to add a few
drops of olive oil to the water to help
prevent sticking.

Timing of pasta cooking is very
important. Follow the directions on
the packet and before stated time is
up, remove a piece and test it. It
should still be firm (al dente). Dried
pasta usually takes 8–12 minutes and
fresh pasta about 3–6 minutes,
depending on the size and thickness.
Drain into a colander immediately.

Pasta is best used as soon as it is
cooked but if you have to keep it
warm for a while, drain and toss with
a little olive oil to keep pieces sepa-
rate. If it is to be used cold in a salad
rinse thoroughly under cold water

after cooking. Drain and toss in a
little oil. Refrigerate.

The recipes in this book use dried
pasta unless fresh pasta is specified.
If you prefer, you can substitute fresh.
Vary the cooking time accordingly.
Amount of pasta per person: For
an average serving you will need
75–125 g (2¹/2–4¹/2 oz) of dried pasta
per person and 125–175 g (4¹/2–6 oz)
of fresh.

*Use a vegetable peeler to shave fresh
Parmesan for garnishes and salads.*

To serve: The traditional way of
serving pasta such as spaghetti or
fettuccine is to divide cooked pasta
into individual serving bowls and
toss with a little of the sauce. The
remaining sauce is then placed in a
bowl at the table so guests can help
themselves.

An easy way to serve is to return
drained, cooked pasta to pan. Add
sauce; toss until combined. Transfer
to large serving bowl or divide
between individual serving dishes.

LONG PASTA

There is an enormous variety of
widths, thicknesses and shapes of
long pasta. Round ones include
spaghetti, vermicelli and spaghettini.
Some, such as bucatini, have a hole
through the middle to allow thin
sauces to flow through.

Spaghetti is often served simply
with oil and garlic. However, it can be
served with any sauce which clings to

the pasta. Vermicelli can be used in
the same way.

Flat, long pasta such as fettuccine,
tagliatelle and linguine are also best
with sauces which cling when strands
are picked up.

Seafood, including mussels, is
often served with long pasta but big,
chunky pieces of vegetables and meat
aren't easy to eat with any of the
long pasta. Bolognaise sauce goes
well with spaghetti and tagliatelle.
To eat: Use a fork to spear a few
strands and place the tip of the fork
against a spoon. Twirl fork so strands
wind around the fork. Or just push
the fork against the plate and twirl.

SHORT PASTA

These are straight or shaped and
sometimes tubular. Tubular and
shaped short pasta retain the accompanying sauce well and are easy to
pick up with most sauces, including
chunky meat and vegetables. All
short pastas are interchangeable.
CONCHIGLIE: Shell-shaped pasta
which comes in various sizes. Large
shells are excellent for baking with
fillings such as seafood whereas small
shells can be used in casseroles and
soups or can be served cold in salads.
FARFALLE: Butterfly- or bow tie-
shaped pasta. Excellent with meat or
vegetable sauces.
FUSILLI: Twist or spiral pasta—good
in salads and with meat sauces as the
meat gets caught in the spirals.
MACARONI: Straight or curved
(elbows) short lengths of pasta with a
hole through the centre. Often used in
baked dishes.
PENNE: Straight short lengths with a
smooth or ridged surface, with a wide
hole through the middle. Ends are cut
at an angle. Retain sauce well.
LASAGNE SHEETS: Flat or ridged
sheets of pasta. Layered with sauces
and then baked. Some need pre-cook-
ing before layering. Follow the manufacturer's instructions.

*Hold one end of long pasta and ease
it into boiling water as it softens.*

FILLED PASTA

CANNELLONI TUBES: Pasta which have a hole big enough for filling with meat and vegetable sauces. After filling, they are baked with a sauce poured over the top to keep them moist.

RAVIOLI AND TORTELLINI: Pasta shapes with a variety of fillings including vegetable, chicken and meat. Buy them fresh or dried or make your own. They are cooked separately and usually served with mild sauces that don't overwhelm the flavour of the filling.

GNOCCHI

Small savoury dumplings made with vegetables or semolina. They are poached and served with sauces.

PASTA FOR SOUPS

Many different shapes are available for adding to soups and casseroles. There are little stars (stelline), small versions of shells (conchiglie) and farfalle (butterflies or bow ties) and even pasta in the shape of letters of the alphabet.

CHEESE

Cheese, most commonly Parmesan, is often used in pasta dishes. Sometimes it is part of the sauce, sometimes simply used as a garnish.

For storage, it is preferable that hard cheeses be wrapped tightly in foil or kitchen paper and refrigerated. If you prefer to use plastic wrap, squeeze out as much air as possible and then wrap in foil as well.

Cheese used in pasta dishes should be freshly grated—avoid ready-grated cheeses.

Soft cheeses such as ricotta are excellent in stuffings because they help bind other ingredients together and have a pleasant texture. Refrigerate in a covered container.

PARMESAN is a hard granular, light yellow cheese with a very strong flavour which blends extremely well with meat, tomato and vegetable sauces as well as some creamy sauces and soups. It is not generally used with mushroom sauces or seafood. Parmesan cheese keeps for months if wrapped tightly before refrigeration.

Parmigiano-reggiano is the best type of Parmesan with a good strong flavour. It is available at most delicatessens. The rind should have its name marked on it. If you can't get it, try *Grana*. If you can't find either of these, use the block Parmesan available from the dairy section of most supermarkets. Avoid ready-grated Parmesan.

GRUYÈRE is a form of firm Swiss cheese, pale yellow in colour. Gruyère varies from dry and strong-flavoured to a more mild creamy style. The creamy one is preferable in most sauces. Gruyère is an excellent melting cheese which draws hardly any threads. You can use a cheddar as a substitute if you prefer.

ROMANO is a hard granular cheese with a biting flavour. It has small holes throughout and is golden yellow, darkening with maturity. Sometimes it is used as a substitute for Parmesan cheese. Like Parmesan, it is often finely grated or shaved for use as a garnish to enhance the flavour of pasta dishes.

PECORINO is a hard granular cheese, pale yellow, darkening with maturity. It has a stronger, more piquant, tangy taste than Parmesan and can be used as a substitute for parmesan if you enjoy the biting flavour. Like Parmesan, it stores for a long time.

RICOTTA is a moist, fine, white cheese with a sweet, delicate flavour. The texture is quite creamy. It is very good for use in the fillings for pasta dishes such as cannelloni and is quite often used in the cooking of sweet dishes.

BOCCONCINI AND OVOLINI are soft, moist, mild, almost white cheeses. Ovolini is a small version of bocconcini. If bought unpackaged from delicatessens, refrigerate in the whey that they come in and use within 3 days. Those sold in sealed bags have a use-by date on them—use within 3 days of opening.

MOZZARELLA is a soft, smooth cheese, pale yellow in colour. It has a mild, sweet flavour and is excellent for recipes that have the cheese melted on top and for use in salads.

GORGONZOLA is a soft, creamy, blue-veined cheese with quite a pungent smell and a strong bite to its taste. It adds richness to pasta dishes but you can choose a milder-flavoured blue cheese, if you prefer a more subtle taste.

CHEDDAR comes in various strengths including mild, semi-matured, matured and vintage. The milder ones are paler yellow in colour. They are all quite firm but the more mature ones are often more crumbly. All the Cheddars are interchangeable.

HERBS

Basil, oregano, rosemary, sage, thyme and parsley are some of the herbs commonly found in pasta recipes. When herbs are stated in recipes, you should consider them as suggestions. If you prefer a different herb, or combination of herbs, experiment and develop your own recipes.

The amount of herbs used for any recipe is also a matter of personal taste. Substitute fresh herbs for dried if you wish but you need about three times as much when using fresh as they are not as strong as dried. Most herbs grow easily in sunny spots in the garden or in hanging baskets or pots.

DRIED PASTA

Dried pasta is commercially prepared and packaged, made from flour, water and salt and sometimes egg. Some shapes are especially suited to a particular type of sauce. Here we have given a guide to suitable sauces but you do not have to stick to any strict rules—it's your choice.

Below: Tagliatelle
(best with thin
coating sauces)

Right: Tomato tagliatelle
(excellent with thin
coating sauces)

Left: Penne
(best with thick or
chunky sauces)

Left: Rigatoni
(best with
chunky or thick
sauces)

Right: Lasagne
(layered with
sauces and baked)

Below: Conchiglie or
shells
(best with chunky
sauces which get trapped
in shells)

Above: Fettuccine
(excellent with thin
coating sauces)

Left: Risoni
(added to soups, casseroles)

Left: Linguine (best with thin coating sauces)

Left: Fusilli (best with sauces which get trapped in grooves)

Left: Orecchiette (best with sauces which get trapped in grooves)

Right: Spaghetti (best with thin coating sauces or bolognaise)

Above: Spiral pasta (best with sauces which get trapped in grooves)

Left: Spinach tagliatelle (best with thin coating sauces)

Below: Macaroni (best in baked dishes, soups)

Above: Farfalle or butterflies (best with sauces which get trapped in grooves)

Above: Tortellini shapes (excellent with sauces which get trapped in grooves)

Above: Cannelloni (stuffed with filling and baked in a sauce)

Above: Ziti (suitable for thick or thin sauces)

Above right: Miniature star-shaped pasta (best for soups)

Above: Macaroni elbows (best in baked dishes, soups)

7

FRESH PASTA

Specialty pasta shops and some supermarkets and delicatessens stock fresh pasta. Some are flavoured with herbs and spices or coloured with vegetables. Fresh pasta cooks a lot more quickly than dried pasta. Here we have suggested types of sauces for each pasta.

Right: Lasagne sheets (layered with thick sauces and baked)

Above: Ravioli (excellent with mild-flavoured thin sauces)

Below: Pumpkin Gnocchi (best with thin sauces)

Left: Tortellini (best with mild-flavoured thin sauces)

Below: Gnocchi (excellent with thin sauces)

Left: Cracked pepper tagliatelle (best with thin coating sauces)

Below: Pumpkin ravioli (best with mild-flavoured thin sauces)

Below right: Spinach gnocchi (best with thin coating sauces)

Below right: Tomato tagliatelle
Below left: Spinach tagliatelle (both are best with thin coating sauces)

Left: Spaghetti (best with thin coating sauces or bolognaise)

Above: Spinach tortellini (excellent with thin sauces)

Above: Pappardelle (suitable for thick, thin or chunky sauces)

9

BASIC SAUCES

TOMATO AND OLIVE SAUCE

Preparation time: 25 minutes
Total cooking time: 15 minutes
Serves 4–6

1 kg (2 lb 4 oz) large ripe
   tomatoes
1 tablespoon olive oil
2 garlic cloves, crushed
1 onion, finely chopped
500 g (1 lb 2 oz) penne, spaghetti,
   fettuccine or your choice

60 g (¹/₂ cup) pitted black olives
2 teaspoons soft brown sugar
1 teaspoon red wine vinegar

➤ MARK A SMALL CROSS in the top of each tomato.
1 Place the tomatoes in boiling water for 1–2 minutes, then plunge in cold water. Peel the skin down from the cross, discard skin. Chop the tomatoes. Heat the oil in a heavy-based pan. Add the garlic and onion and cook, stirring, for 5 minutes over low heat.
2 Add the tomatoes, cook, stirring, for

2–3 minutes. Cool slightly. Meanwhile, add the pasta to a large pan of boiling water and cook until just tender. Drain; return to pan.
3 To the cooled sauce, add the olives, sugar, vinegar, salt and pepper to taste and stir until combined. Combine the pasta and sauce. Serve.

COOK'S FILE

Storage time: This sauce can be made up to a day in advance and refrigerated in an airtight container.
Note: If you prefer, you can purée the mixture to a smooth consistency.

TOMATO SAUCE

Preparation time: 15 minutes
Total cooking time: 20 minutes
Serves 4–6

1.5 kg (3 lb 5 oz) large ripe
   tomatoes
1 tablespoon olive oil
2 garlic cloves, crushed
1 onion, chopped
1 carrot, finely chopped
2 tablespoons tomato paste
   (purée)

1 teaspoon sugar
15 g (¼ cup) freshly chopped
   mixed oregano, parsley and
   basil
500 g (1 lb 2 oz) rigatoni, penne,
   spaghetti or your choice

➤ MARK A SMALL CROSS in the
top of each tomato.
1 Place the tomatoes in boiling water
for 1–2 minutes, then plunge into cold
water. Peel the skin down from cross
and discard; roughly chop the tomato.
2 Heat the oil in a pan. Add the garlic
and onion; cook for 5 minutes over low
heat. Add the tomato and carrot; cook,
stirring occasionally, for 10 minutes.
Add the paste, sugar, salt and pepper.
Bring to the boil; cook for 2 minutes.
3 Place the mixture in a food processor and process briefly until the sauce
reaches a desired consistency. Stir in
the herbs. Meanwhile, add the pasta to
a large pan of rapidly boiling water;
cook until just tender. Drain and
return to the pan. Combine with sauce.

COOK'S FILE

Storage time: Refrigerate the sauce
up to 3 days or freeze up to 3 months.

1

2

3

GARLIC SAUCE WITH PARSLEY

Preparation time: 10 minutes
Total cooking time: 15 minutes
Serves 4–6

4 garlic cloves
500 g (1 lb 2 oz) fusilli or spiral pasta
250 ml (1 cup) olive oil
15 g (¼ cup) chopped parsley

➤ CRUSH OR FINELY chop the garlic into a small bowl.

1 Add the pasta to a large pan of boiling water and cook until just tender. Drain pasta and return to pan.

2 About five minutes before pasta is cooked, heat oil in a heavy-based pan over low heat. Add garlic to pan; cook 30 seconds or until garlic is soft.

3 Pour oil and garlic over hot pasta. Add chopped parsley, salt and pepper to taste; toss until pasta is well coated. Serve immediately.

COOK'S FILE

Hint: Cook the garlic until golden brown but not any darker as it will turn bitter.

Buy fresh plump garlic, not old, dried out bulbs.

Variations: Add 150 g (1 cup) chopped olives with the parsley.

Add 2 tablespoons of chopped fresh oregano, basil, chives or sage with the parsley.

Add 4 chopped anchovies when cooking the garlic.

25 MINUTE BOLOGNAISE

Preparation time: 10 minutes
Total cooking time: 25 minutes
Serves 4–6

1 tablespoon olive oil
1 onion, chopped
2 rashers bacon, chopped
1 carrot, grated
750 g (1 lb 10 oz) minced
    (ground) beef

125 g (¹/₂ cup) tomato paste
    (purée)
425 g (15 oz) can tomatoes
1 teaspoon dried mixed herbs
500 g (1 lb 2 oz) spaghetti or
    tagliatelle

➤ HEAT OIL IN A large deep pan. Add the onion, bacon and carrot and stir for 5 minutes over medium heat.
1 Add the beef, breaking up any lumps with the back of a fork. Cook until meat is well browned.

2 Stir in tomato paste, undrained, crushed tomatoes and herbs. Bring to the boil; reduce heat and simmer, uncovered, for 15 minutes, or until meat is tender. Season.
3 Meanwhile, add pasta to a large pan of boiling water and cook until just tender. Drain well. Serve over pasta. Sprinkle with Parmesan cheese.

COOK'S FILE

Note: If desired, use chopped mixed fresh herbs—about 2 tablespoons.

BOLOGNAISE SAUCE

Preparation time: 15 minutes
Total cooking time: 1 hour 30 minutes
Serves 4–6

2 tablespoons olive oil
2 garlic cloves, crushed
1 large onion, chopped
1 carrot, chopped
1 stick celery, chopped
500 g (1 lb 2 oz) minced
  (ground) beef
500 ml (2 cups) beef stock
375 ml (1¹/₂ cups) red wine
2 x 425 g (15 oz) cans tomatoes
1 teaspoon sugar
2 tablespoons chopped parsley

500 g (1 lb 2 oz) spaghetti or
  tagliatelle
2 tablespoons freshly grated
  Parmesan cheese, for serving

➤ HEAT OIL in a large deep pan.
1 Add garlic, onion, carrot and celery. Cook, stirring, for 5 minutes over low heat until golden.
2 Increase heat; add beef, breaking it up with a fork as it cooks. Stir until well browned. Add stock, wine, undrained, crushed tomatoes, sugar and parsley.
3 Bring to the boil; reduce heat and simmer uncovered for 1¹/₂ hours, stir-

ring occasionally. Season with salt and pepper. Meanwhile, add pasta to a pan of rapidly boiling water; cook until just tender. Drain well. Serve sauce over top of pasta. Sprinkle with Parmesan cheese.

COOK'S FILE

Note: Sauce can be used cold for layering in a lasagne. Make a day ahead and store, covered, in refrigerator.

PESTO SAUCE

Preparation time: 10 minutes
Total cooking time: Nil
Serves 4–6

500 g (1 lb 2 oz) tagliatelle or
    fettuccine
40 g (¹/4 cup) pine nuts
100 g (2 cups) basil leaves

2 garlic cloves, crushed
¹/2 teaspoon salt
25 g (¹/4 cup) freshly grated
    Parmesan cheese
2 tablespoons freshly grated
    pecorino cheese (optional)
125 ml (¹/2 cup) olive oil

➤ ADD PASTA to a large pan of rapidly boiling water and cook until just tender. Drain and return to pan.

1 About 5 minutes before pasta is cooked, add pine nuts to a heavy-based pan and stir over low heat for 2–3 minutes or until golden. Cool.
2 Place pine nuts, basil, garlic and salt in food processor and process for 10 seconds. Scrape down the sides.
3 Add the cheeses and process for 10 seconds. With the motor running, gradually add the oil until a paste is formed. Season with pepper. Add to the warm pasta and toss until the sauce coats the pasta.

COOK'S FILE

Storage time: Pesto sauce can be made up to 1 week in advance and stored in an airtight container in the refrigerator.

FAST PASTA

SPAGHETTI WITH PEAS AND BABY ONIONS

Preparation time: 10 minutes
Total cooking time: 15–20 minutes
Serves 4–6

500 g (1 lb 2 oz) spaghetti or
   vermicelli
2 bunches baby onions
1 tablespoon olive oil
4 rashers bacon, chopped
2 teaspoons plain (all-purpose)
   flour
250 ml (1 cup) light chicken
   stock
125 ml (1/2 cup) white wine
155 g (1 cup) shelled fresh peas
fresh oregano sprigs, to garnish
   (optional)

➤ ADD PASTA to a large pan of rapidly boiling water and cook until just tender. Drain pasta well and return to pan.

1 Meanwhile, trim the outer skins and ends from the baby onions, leaving only a small section of the green stem attached.
2 Heat the oil in a large heavy-based deep pan. Add the bacon and baby onions and stir over low heat for 4 minutes, or until golden. Sprinkle the flour lightly over the top and stir for 1 minute.
3 Add the combined stock and wine, increase the heat and bring to the boil.
4 Add the peas and cook for 5 minutes, or until the onions are tender. Season with black pepper. Gently combine the sauce and pasta. Serve in warmed pasta bowls. Garnish with oregano sprigs, if desired.

COOK'S FILE

Hints: Oregano is easy to grow so plant some in your garden or in pots.
   If fresh peas are not available, use frozen ones.
   Very small pickling onions can be used if baby onions are not available.

FETTUCCINE WITH SPINACH AND PROSCIUTTO

Preparation time: 10 minutes
Total cooking time: 10–15 minutes
Serves 4–6

500 g (1 lb 2 oz) spinach or
    plain fettuccine
2 tablespoons olive oil
8 thin slices prosciutto, chopped
3 spring onions (scallions),
    chopped

1 bunch English spinach
1 tablespoon balsamic vinegar
1/2 teaspoon caster (superfine)
    sugar
50 g (1/2 cup) freshly grated
    Parmesan cheese, for serving

➤ ADD PASTA to a large pan of rapidly boiling water and cook until just tender. Drain and return to pan.
1 Meanwhile, heat the oil in a large heavy-based deep pan. Add the prosciutto and spring onion and cook, stirring occasionally, over medium heat for 5 minutes, or until crisp.

2 Trim stalks from the spinach, roughly chop the leaves and add to pan. Stir in the vinegar and sugar, cover and cook 1 minute, or until spinach has softened. Season.
3 Combine the sauce and pasta. Sprinkle with Parmesan and serve.

COOK'S FILE

Storage time: This dish should be served as soon as it is cooked as the spinach turns an unattractive dull dark green if left standing.
Variation: Smoked bacon can be used instead of prosciutto.

FETTUCCINE WITH ZUCCHINI

Preparation time: 15 minutes
Total cooking time: 15 minutes
Serves 4–6

500 g (1 lb 2 oz) tagliatelle or
   fettuccine
60 g (2¼ oz) butter
2 garlic cloves, crushed
500 g (1 lb 2 oz) zucchini
   (courgettes), grated

75 g (³/4 cup) freshly grated
   Parmesan cheese
250 ml (1 cup) olive oil
16 medium-sized basil leaves

➤ COOK PASTA in a large pan of rapidly boiling water until just tender. Drain and return to pan.

1 Meanwhile, heat butter in a deep heavy-based pan over low heat until butter is foaming. Add the garlic and cook for 1 minute. Add the zucchini and cook, stirring occasionally, for 1–2 minutes, or until softened.

2 Add the sauce and Parmesan to the pasta and toss well.

3 To make basil leaves crisp, heat the oil in a small pan, cook 2 leaves at a time for 1 minute, or until crisp. Remove with a slotted spoon and drain on paper towels. Repeat. Serve the pasta in warmed bowls, garnished with the crisp basil leaves.

C O O K ' S   F I L E

Hint: Basil leaves can be fried up to 2 hours in advance. Store in an air-tight container after cooling.

1

2

3

LINGUINE WITH RED PEPPER SAUCE

Preparation time: 20 minutes
Total cooking time: 30 minutes
Serves 4–6

3 red capsicum (peppers)
3 tablespoons olive oil
1 large onion, sliced
2 garlic cloves, crushed
1/4–1/2 teaspoon chilli flakes
 or powder
125 ml (1/2 cup) whipping or
 thick (double/heavy) cream
2 tablespoons chopped fresh
 oregano

500 g (1 lb 2 oz) linguine or
 spaghetti, plain or spinach

➤ HALVE EACH CAPSICUM and
use a sharp knife to remove all the
membrane and seeds.
1 Place the capsicum cut-side down
under a hot grill (broiler) and cook for
8 minutes, or until black and blistered.
Cover with a damp tea towel and
allow to cool. Peel off the skin and cut
the capsicum into thin strips.
2 Heat the oil in large heavy-based
pan. Add the sliced onion and cook,
stirring, over low heat for 8 minutes,
or until soft. Add the capsicum strips,
garlic, chilli and cream and cook for
2 minutes, stirring occasionally. Add

the chopped oregano and season to
taste with salt and freshly ground
black pepper.
3 Before the sauce is cooked, add the
pasta to a large pan of rapidly boiling
water and cook until just tender.
Drain pasta well and return to pan.
Add the sauce to the hot pasta and
toss until well combined. Serve in
warmed pasta bowls.

COOK'S FILE

Hint: If necessary, you can substitute
dried oregano—use about one-third of
the quantity as dried herbs have a
much stronger flavour.
Variation: For a stronger capsicum
flavour, omit the cream.

SPIRALS WITH GREEN SAUCE

Preparation time: 10 minutes
Total cooking time: 15 minutes
Serves 4–6

500 g (1 lb 2 oz) fusilli or spiral
 pasta
1 onion
2 zucchini (courgettes)
5–6 large silverbeet (Swiss chard)
 leaves
2 anchovies
1 tablespoon capers

2 tablespoons olive oil
50 g (1 3/4 oz) butter
60 ml (1/4 cup) white wine

➤ ADD PASTA to a large pan of boiling water and cook until just tender.
Drain and return to pan.
1 Meanwhile, finely chop the onion
and grate the zucchini. Remove and
discard the stalks from silverbeet.
Chop or shred the leaves into small
pieces. Chop the anchovies and capers
finely. Heat the oil and butter in a
large heavy-based deep pan. Add the
onion and zucchini and cook, stirring,
for 3 minutes over medium heat.

2 Add the anchovies, capers and
wine. Season with salt and pepper and
cook, stirring, for 2 minutes.
3 Add the silverbeet to the pan and
cook for 1–2 minutes, or until the
silverbeet softens. Add the sauce to
the warm pasta and toss until well
distributed. Serve immediately in
warmed pasta bowls.

COOK'S FILE

Note: Filleted anchovies are available
canned in oil or salted in jars.
Variation: Use a whole bunch of
English spinach instead of silverbeet.
Cut ends off; shred into small pieces.

Linguine with Red Pepper Sauce (top) and
Spirals with Green Sauce

GRILLED CAPSICUM AND ANCHOVY SALAD

Preparation time: 15 minutes
Total cooking time: 25 minutes
Serves 4–6

500 g (1 lb 2 oz) penne or spiral
    pasta
1 small red onion
2 large red capsicum (peppers)
80 g (1 cup) fresh flat-leaf
    (Italian) parsley leaves
2 anchovies, whole or chopped
60 ml (¼ cup) olive oil
2 tablespoons lemon juice

➤ ADD PENNE OR SPIRAL pasta to
a large pan of rapidly boiling water
and cook until just tender.

1 Drain the pasta immediately and
rinse well under cold water. Chop the
onion finely.

2 Cut the capsicum in half and
remove the seeds and membrane.
Place cut-side down under a hot grill
(broiler) and cook for 8 minutes, or
until skin is blistered and black. Cover
with a damp tea towel. When cool,
peel the skin away and cut the flesh
into thin strips.

3 In a large salad bowl, combine the
pasta, capsicum strips, onion, parsley,
anchovies, oil and lemon juice. Season
with salt and pepper. Toss until well
combined and serve immediately.

COOK'S FILE

Hints: To prevent the pasta sticking
together, after rinsing under cold
water add a little of the oil to the pasta
and toss well.

    Capsicum can be prepared a day in
advance, covered well and then refrigerated. Removing the skin in this way
results in a much sweeter taste from
the capsicum.

1

2

3

SPAGHETTI TOMATO SALAD

Preparation time: 25 minutes
Total cooking time: 15 minutes
Serves 4–6

500 g (1 lb 2 oz) spaghettini or
  spaghetti
50 g (1 cup) fresh basil leaves
250 g (9 oz) cherry tomatoes,
  halved
1 garlic clove, crushed

75 g (¹/₂ cup) chopped black
  olives
60 ml (¹/₄ cup) olive oil
1 tablespoon balsamic vinegar
50 g (¹/₂ cup) freshly grated
  Parmesan cheese

➤ ADD PASTA to a large pan of
rapidly boiling water and cook until
just tender. Drain pasta and rinse well
under cold water.
1 Using a sharp knife, chop the basil
leaves into fine strips.
2 Combine the basil, tomato, garlic,

olives, oil and vinegar. Allow to stand
for 15 minutes. Place the pasta in a
large salad bowl; add tomato mixture.
3 Add the Parmesan, season and toss
well. Serve immediately.

COOK'S FILE

Storage time: Pasta can be cooked
up to 1 day in advance. If doing this,
cool pasta and toss with a little oil.
Note: Balsamic vinegar is an aged
vinegar from Modena, Italy. It is
available in delicatessens and some
supermarkets.

1

2

3

FARFALLE SALAD WITH SUNDRIED TOMATOES AND SPINACH

Preparation time: 20 minutes
Total cooking time: 12 minutes
Serves 4–6

500 g (1 lb 2 oz) farfalle (butterfly pasta) or spiral pasta
3 spring onions (scallions)

50 g (1³/4 oz) sundried (sun-blushed) tomatoes, cut into strips
1 bunch English spinach, stalks trimmed and leaves shredded
50 g (¹/3 cup) toasted pine nuts
1 tablespoon chopped fresh oregano

Dressing
60 ml (¹/4 cup) olive oil
1 teaspoon fresh chopped chilli
1 garlic clove, crushed

➤ ADD PASTA to a large saucepan of rapidly boiling water and cook until just tender. Drain the pasta and rinse well under cold water. Transfer to a large salad bowl.

1 Trim the spring onions and chop finely. Add to the pasta with sundried tomato, spinach, pine nuts and oregano.

2 To make Dressing: Combine the oil, chilli and garlic in a small screw-top jar. Season, then shake well.

3 Pour the dressing over the salad; toss well and serve immediately.

1

2

3

ITALIAN OMELETTE

Preparation time: 20 minutes
Total cooking time: 15 minutes
Serves 4

2 tablespoons olive oil
1 onion, finely chopped
125 g (4¹/2 oz) ham, sliced
6 eggs
60 ml (¹/4 cup) milk
350 g (2 cups) cooked spiral pasta
　　(150 g/5¹/2 oz uncooked)

25 g (¹/4 cup) freshly grated
　　Parmesan cheese
2 tablespoons chopped fresh
　　parsley
1 tablespoon chopped fresh basil
60 g (¹/2 cup) freshly grated
　　Cheddar cheese

➤ HEAT HALF the oil in a pan. Add the onion and stir over low heat until tender.

1 Add the ham to the pan and stir for 1 minute, then transfer to a plate.

2 In a bowl, whisk the eggs and milk together, then season with salt and pepper. Stir in the pasta, Parmesan, herbs and onion mixture.

3 Heat the remaining oil in the same pan, then pour in the egg mixture. Sprinkle with the cheese. Cook over medium heat until mixture begins to set around the edges. Place under a hot grill (broiler) to complete the cooking. Cut into wedges to serve.

COOK'S FILE

Hint: Serve with a crisp green or mixed salad, if desired.

1

2

3

PASTA WITH RICOTTA, CHILLI AND HERBS

Preparation time: 15 minutes
Total cooking time: 20 minutes
Serves 4

500 g (1 lb 2 oz) spiral pasta or
   penne
60 ml (¹/₄ cup) olive oil
3 garlic cloves, crushed
2 teaspoons finely chopped chilli

60 g (1 cup) fresh flat-leaf
   (Italian) parsley, chopped
30 g (¹/₂ cup) fresh basil leaves,
   shredded
20 g (¹/₂ cup) fresh oregano
   leaves, roughly chopped
200 g (7 oz) fresh ricotta
   cheese, cut into small cubes

➤ ADD PASTA to a large pan of rapidly boiling water and cook until just tender. Drain and return to pan.
1 When the pasta is almost cooked, heat the oil in a non-stick heavy-based frying pan. Add the garlic and chilli and stir for 1 minute over low heat.
2 Add the oil mixture and herbs to the pasta. Season to taste with salt and black pepper. Toss until the mixture coats the pasta thoroughly.
3 Add the cubes of ricotta and serve immediately.

COOK'S FILE

Note: Fresh ricotta cheese is sold in delicatessens. Use within 2 days.

GREEN OLIVE AND EGGPLANT TOSS

Preparation time: 20 minutes
Total cooking time: 20 minutes
Serves 4

**500 g (1 lb 2 oz) fettuccine or
tagliatelle**
175 g (1 cup) green olives
1 large eggplant (aubergine)
2 tablespoons olive oil

2 garlic cloves, crushed
125 ml (¹/2 cup) lemon juice
**2 tablespoons chopped fresh
parsley**
**50 g (¹/2 cup) freshly grated
Parmesan cheese**

➤ ADD PASTA to a large pan of rapidly boiling water and cook until just tender. Drain and return to pan.
1 Meanwhile, chop the olives and cut the eggplant into small cubes.
2 Heat the oil in a frying pan. Add

the garlic; stir for 30 seconds. Add the eggplant and cook over medium heat, stirring frequently, for 6 minutes, or until tender.
3 Add the olives and lemon juice. Season. Add the sauce to the pasta and toss. Serve in warmed bowls. Sprinkle with the parsley and cheese.

C O O K ' S F I L E

Hint: To draw out bitter juices, eggplant can be salted, left to stand for 30 minutes, then rinsed.

Spaghetti with Rocket and Chilli

Tagliatelle with Herb Sauce

Spiral Pasta with Breadcrumb Sauce

PRONTO PASTA

SPAGHETTI WITH ROCKET AND CHILLI

Add 500 g (1 lb 2 oz) spaghetti or spaghettini to a large pan of rapidly boiling water and cook until just tender. Drain and return to pan. Five minutes before pasta is cooked, heat 2 tablespoons olive oil in a large heavy-based frying pan. Add 2 teaspoons chopped chilli and cook for 1 minute over low heat, stirring. Add 3 bunches trimmed rocket (arugula) and cook for 2–3 minutes or until softened, stirring regularly. Add 1 tablespoon lemon juice and salt, to taste. Add sauce to pasta and toss until mixed. Serve. Serves 4–6.

SPIRAL PASTA WITH BREADCRUMB SAUCE

Process 5 slices brown bread in a food processor for 30 seconds or until it forms fine crumbs. Add 500 g (1 lb 2 oz) spiral pasta or farfalle to a large pan of rapidly boiling water and cook until just tender. Drain, keep warm. While pasta is cooking, heat 60 ml ($1/4$ cup) olive oil in a large heavy-based frying pan over low heat. Add breadcrumbs and 3 cloves crushed garlic and stir 3 minutes or until crisp and golden. Combine hot pasta, breadcrumbs, 2 tablespoons finely chopped parsley and 45 g($1/2$ cup) freshly grated pecorino cheese in a large serving bowl. Add ground black pepper, to taste. Toss well and serve immediately. Garnish with fresh herbs, if desired. Serves 4–6.

Shells with Artichoke,
Salami and Tomato

Lasagnette with Spinach
and Mushroom Sauce

LASAGNETTE WITH SPINACH AND MUSHROOM SAUCE

Add 500 g (1 lb 2 oz) lasagnette or pappardelle to a large pan of rapidly boiling water and cook until just tender. Drain and return to pan. Meanwhile, heat 2 tablespoons olive oil and 60 g (2¼ oz) butter in a large heavy-based pan over medium heat. Add 3 chopped spring onions (scallions) and 250 g (9 oz) sliced baby mushrooms and cook for 5 minutes, stirring occasionally, over medium heat. Add 1 bunch English spinach, stems removed and leaves shredded, and cook 2 minutes, or until spinach is just tender. Season to taste. Add the sauce to the pasta and toss until combined. Divide the pasta among warmed serving bowls. Garnish with freshly grated Parmesan cheese and serve immediately. Serves 4–6.

TAGLIATELLE WITH HERB SAUCE

Add 500 g (1 lb 2 oz) tagliatelle or trenette to a large pan of rapidly boiling water and cook until just tender. Drain and return to pan. Meanwhile, place 30 g (1½ cups) fresh parsley, 50 g (1 cup) fresh basil leaves, 15 g (½ cup) fresh oregano and 40 g (¼ cup) toasted pine nuts in a food processor and process for 10 seconds, or until finely chopped. With the motor running, add 125 ml (½ cup) olive oil and process for 10 seconds, or until it forms a smooth paste. Season to taste. Add the sauce to the pasta and toss well. Serve immediately, garnished with shavings of fresh Parmesan cheese, if desired. Serves 4–6.

SHELLS WITH ARTICHOKE, SALAMI AND TOMATO

Add 500 g (1 lb 2 oz) shells or spiral pasta to a large pan of rapidly boiling water and cook until just tender. Drain, keep warm. Heat 2 tablespoons olive oil in a large heavy-based frying pan; add 6 slices salami, cut into strips, and stir for 2 minutes over medium heat. Stir in 10 sundried (sun-blushed) tomatoes, cut into strips. Drain 425 g (15 oz) can artichoke hearts, cut into wedges. Add to pan with pepper, to taste, and 2 tablespoons each of chopped fresh basil and parsley; cook for 1 minute. Divide pasta among warmed serving bowls and top with the sauce. Serves 4–6.

SOUPS

BEAN SOUP WITH SAUSAGE

Preparation time: 25 minutes
Total cooking time: 25 minutes
Serves 4–6

4 Italian sausages
2 teaspoons olive oil
2 medium leeks, sliced
1 garlic clove, crushed
1 large carrot, chopped into
    small cubes
2 sticks celery, sliced
2 tablespoons plain (all-purpose)
    flour
2 beef stock cubes, crumbled
2 litres (8 cups) hot water
125 ml (1/2 cup) white wine
125 g (41/2 oz) small shell
    pasta
440 g (151/2 oz) can three bean
    mix, drained
1 teaspoon chopped chilli
    (optional)

➤ CUT SAUSAGES into small pieces.

1 Heat oil in a large heavy-based pan and add sausage pieces. Cook over medium heat for 5 minutes or until golden, stirring regularly. Remove from pan and drain on paper towels.

2 Add leek, garlic, carrot and celery to pan, cook for 2–3 minutes or until soft, stirring occasionally.

3 Add flour, cook 1 minute stirring constantly. Add stock cubes; gradually stir in water and wine. Bring to boil; reduce heat; simmer, uncovered, 10 minutes.

4 Add pasta, beans and chilli to pan. Increase heat; cook 8–10 minutes or until pasta is tender. Return sausage to pan, add salt and pepper. Serve with chopped fresh parsley, if desired.

COOK'S FILE

Variation: Use dried beans, if preferred. Place in a bowl; cover with water; soak overnight. Drain; add to large pan with enough water to cover beans by 3 cm (11/4 inch); simmer for 1 hour. Drain well, then add to soup.

MINESTRONE WITH PESTO

Preparation time: 25 minutes
Total cooking time: 30 minutes
Serves 4–6

2 onions, chopped
1 green capsicum (pepper),
    membrane and seeds
    removed, chopped
2 large zucchini (courgettes),
    sliced
1 small eggplant (aubergine),
    chopped
2 large carrots, chopped

2 beef stock cubes, crumbled
155 g (1 cup) frozen peas
440 g (15¹/₂ oz) can borlotti or
    kidney beans, drained
250 g (9 oz) miniature pasta
15 g (¹/₄ cup) chopped fresh
    parsley
2 tablespoons freshly grated
    Parmesan cheese, for serving

Pesto
2 garlic cloves, crushed
100 g (2 cups) fresh basil
    leaves
50 g (¹/₂ cup) freshly grated
    Parmesan cheese
125 ml (¹/₂ cup) olive oil

▶ PLACE THE onion, capsicum, zucchini, eggplant, carrot in large deep pan with 2 litres (8 cups) hot water.

1 Add the crumbled stock cubes. Bring to the boil over high heat, then reduce the heat and simmer for 20 minutes, stirring occasionally.

2 Add the peas, beans, pasta and parsley. Cook for 10 minutes, or until the pasta is just tender. Season to taste with salt and pepper. Serve with the pesto. Sprinkle with freshly grated Parmesan cheese.

3 To make Pesto: Combine the garlic, basil, cheese and oil in a food processor and process for 10 seconds or until mixture forms a paste.

1

2

3

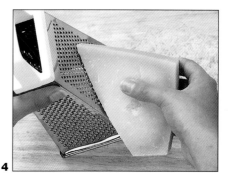

LEMON-SCENTED BROTH WITH TORTELLINI

Preparation time: 10 minutes
Total cooking time: 18 minutes
Serves 4–6

1 lemon
125 ml (¹/₂ cup) good quality
   white wine
440 g (15¹/₂ oz) can chicken
   consomme
20 g (¹/₃ cup) chopped fresh
   parsley
375 g (13 oz) fresh or dried
   veal- or chicken-filled
   tortellini

2 tablespoons freshly grated
   Parmesan cheese (optional)

➤ USING A VEGETABLE peeler, peel wide strips from the lemon.

1 Remove any white pith with a small sharp knife, then cut 3 of the wide pieces into fine strips; set aside the fine strips to garnish.

2 Place the wide lemon strips, wine, consomme and 750 ml (3 cups) water in a large saucepan. Cook for 10 minutes over low heat. Remove the lemon rind and bring mixture to the boil.

3 Add 2 tablespoons of parsley and tortellini to the pan. Season, then cook for 6–7 minutes, or until pasta is just tender. Garnish with the remaining parsley and fine strips of lemon rind.

4 Sprinkle with grated Parmesan, if desired.

COOK'S FILE

Storage time: If desired, the day before broth is required, follow recipe to the removal of lemon rind from pan. Just before serving, bring mixture to the boil; add chopped parsley, black pepper and tortellini. Continue with recipe.

COUNTRY PUMPKIN AND PASTA SOUP

Preparation time: 25 minutes
Total cooking time: 18 minutes
Serves 4–6

1 large onion
700 g (1 lb 9 oz) pumpkin
2 potatoes
1 tablespoon olive oil
30 g (1 oz) butter

2 garlic cloves, crushed
3 litres (12 cups) light chicken stock
125 g (4¹/₂ oz) miniature pasta or risoni
1 tablespoon chopped fresh parsley, to serve (optional)

➤ PEEL ONION and chop finely.

1 Peel pumpkin and potatoes and chop into small cubes. Heat oil and butter in a large pan. Add the onion and garlic and cook, stirring, for 5 minutes over low heat.

2 Add the pumpkin, potato and stock. Increase the heat, cover the pan and cook for 8 minutes, or until the vegetables are tender.

3 Add the pasta and cook, stirring occasionally, for 5 minutes, or until pasta is just tender. Serve immediately. Sprinkle with chopped parsley.

COOK'S FILE

Note: Butternut (squash) or Japanese pumpkin gives the sweetest flavour.

1

2

3

BACON AND PEA SOUP

Preparation time: 20 minutes
Total cooking time: 15 minutes
Serves 4–6

1 large onion
4 rashers bacon
50 g (1³/4 oz) butter
1 stick celery, chopped into
    small pieces
2 litres (8 cups) chicken stock

155 g (1 cup) frozen peas
250 g (9 oz) risoni
2 tablespoons chopped fresh
    parsley

➤ PEEL ONION and chop finely.
1 Trim the rind and excess fat from the bacon, then chop the bacon into small pieces.
2 Place the bacon, butter, onion and celery in large heavy-based pan. Cook for 5 minutes over low heat, stirring occasionally. Add the stock and peas, and simmer, covered, for 5 minutes. Increase the heat and add pasta. Cook, uncovered, stirring occasionally, for 5 minutes.
3 Add the chopped parsley and season with ground black pepper just before serving.

COOK'S FILE

Storage time: You can make this soup the day before required and store in an airtight container in refrigerator. Gently reheat before serving.

PASTA WITH TOMATO

SPAGHETTI PUTTANESCA

Preparation time: 15 minutes
Total cooking time: 20 minutes
Serves 4–6

500 g (1 lb 2 oz) spaghetti or
    fettuccine
2 tablespoons olive oil
3 garlic cloves, crushed
2 tablespoons chopped fresh
    parsley
1/4–1/2 teaspoon chilli flakes or
    powder
2 x 425 g (15 oz) can tomatoes
1 tablespoon capers
3 anchovy fillets, chopped
45 g (1/4 cup) black olives

➤ ADD SPAGHETTI or fettuccine to
a large pan of rapidly boiling water.

1 Cook pasta until just tender and
drain immediately. Return drained
pasta to pan.
2 While pasta is cooking, heat oil in a
heavy-based frying pan. Add garlic,
parsley and chilli flakes and cook,
stirring, 1 minute over medium heat.
3 Add undrained, crushed tomatoes
and stir to combine. Reduce heat and
simmer, covered, for 5 minutes.
4 Add capers, anchovies and olives
and cook, stirring, for 5 minutes. Add
black pepper; stir. Add sauce to pasta
and toss gently until evenly distributed. Serve immediately in warmed
pasta bowls.

COOK'S FILE

Hint: You can leave tomatoes in the
can and chop with a pair of kitchen
scissors. Otherwise, drain them,
reserving juice, and chop on a board.

BUCATINI WITH FARMHOUSE SAUCE

Preparation time: 20 minutes
Total cooking time: 25 minutes
Serves 4–6

2 tablespoons olive oil
250 g (9 oz) mushrooms
1 eggplant (aubergine)
2 garlic cloves, crushed
825 g (1 lb 13 oz) can tomatoes, crushed

500 g (1 lb 2 oz) bucatini or spaghetti
15 g (1/4 cup) chopped fresh parsley

➤ HEAT OIL in a medium heavy-based pan.
1 Wipe the mushrooms with paper towels, then cut into slices. Chop the eggplant into small cubes.
2 Add the mushrooms, eggplant and garlic to the pan and cook, stirring, for 4 minutes. Add the tomatoes, then cover and simmer for 15 minutes.

Meanwhile, add the pasta to a large saucepan of rapidly boiling water and cook until just tender. Drain and return to the pan.
3 Season the sauce with salt and ground black pepper, then stir in the parsley. Add the sauce to the pasta and toss well. Serve immediately in warmed pasta bowls.

COOK'S FILE

Hint: If the pasta is cooked before you are ready to serve, toss a little olive oil through it after draining.

1

2

3

RIGATONI WITH KIDNEY BEANS AND ITALIAN SAUSAGE

Preparation time: 25 minutes
Total cooking time: 30 minutes
Serves 4–6

1 tablespoon olive oil
1 large onion, chopped
2 garlic cloves, crushed
4 Italian sausages, chopped
825 g (1 lb 13 oz) can tomatoes
425 g (15 oz) can kidney or
   borlotti beans, drained

2 tablespoons chopped fresh
   basil
1 tablespoon chopped fresh sage
1 tablespoon chopped fresh
   parsley
500 g (1 lb 2 oz) rigatoni or
   large shells
25 g ($^1/4$ cup) freshly grated
   Parmesan cheese, to serve

➤ HEAT OIL in a medium heavy-based pan.
1 Add the onion, garlic and sausage to the pan and cook, stirring occasionally, over medium heat for 5 minutes.
2 Add undrained, crushed tomatoes, beans, basil, sage and parsley. Season with salt and pepper. Reduce the heat and simmer for 20 minutes.
3 Meanwhile, add the pasta to a large saucepan of boiling water and cook until just tender. Drain. Divide the pasta among warmed serving bowls, top with the sauce. Sprinkle with the Parmesan and serve immediately.

COOK'S FILE

Hint: Dried beans may be used. Soak overnight in water; drain, place in a pan, cover well with water, bring to the boil and cook for 20 minutes or until tender.

PENNE WITH PROSCIUTTO

Preparation time: 15 minutes
Total cooking time: 25 minutes
Serves 4–6

1 onion
825 g (1 lb 13 oz) can tomatoes
1 tablespoon olive oil
6 thin slices prosciutto
    (approximately 70 g/2½ oz),
    chopped
1 tablespoon chopped fresh
    rosemary
500 g (1 lb 2 oz) penne or
    macaroni
50 g (½ cup) freshly grated
    Parmesan cheese, to serve

➤ PEEL ONION and chop finely.
1 Using scissors, crush the tomatoes while still in the can.
2 Heat the oil in a heavy-based frying pan. Add the prosciutto and onion and cook, stirring occasionally, over low heat for 5 minutes, or until golden.

3 Add the rosemary and tomatoes. Season, then simmer for 10 minutes. While the sauce is cooking, add the pasta to a large pan of rapidly boiling water and cook until just tender. Drain. Divide the pasta among warmed serving bowls and top with the sauce. Sprinkle with the Parmesan and serve immediately.

COOK'S FILE

Note: Rosemary, commonly used in Mediterranean cookery, adds a distinctive flavour to this dish.

1

2

3

RIGATONI WITH AMATRICIANA SAUCE

Preparation time: 25 minutes
Total cooking time: 20 minutes
Serves 4–6

1 kg (2 lb 4 oz) ripe tomatoes
500 g (1 lb 2 oz) rigatoni
1 tablespoon olive oil
3 thin slices bacon or 6 thin slices pancetta, finely chopped
1 small onion, very finely chopped
2 teaspoons very finely chopped fresh chilli

► MARK A SMALL CROSS in the bottom of each tomato.
1 Place the tomatoes in boiling water for 1–2 minutes, then plunge into cold water. Remove from the water, then peel the skin down from the cross. Roughly chop the flesh.
2 Add rigatoni to a large saucepan of rapidly boiling water and cook until just tender. Drain and return to pan. Keep warm.
3 About 6 minutes before the rigatoni is cooked, heat the oil in a heavy-based frying pan. Add the bacon, onion and chilli and stir over medium heat for 3 minutes. Add the tomato, and season with salt and ground black pepper. Reduce the heat and simmer for 3 minutes. Add sauce to pasta and toss until well combined.

COOK'S FILE

Hint: Try Roma or egg tomatoes in this recipe—you'll find them sometimes in supermarkets or greengrocers. They are firm-fleshed, with few seeds and a rich flavour. Use them in sauces and for bottling and sun-drying—they are particularly good.

1

2

3

SPAGHETTI SIRACUSANI

Preparation time: 15 minutes
Total cooking time: 1 hour
Serves 4–6

1 large green capsicum (pepper)
2 tablespoons olive oil
2 garlic cloves, crushed
2 x 425 g (15 oz) cans tomatoes,
   crushed
2 zucchini (courgettes), chopped
2 anchovy fillets, chopped
1 tablespoon capers, chopped

45 g ($^1/_4$ cup) black olives,
   pitted and halved
2 tablespoons chopped fresh
   basil leaves
500 g (1 lb 2 oz) spaghetti or
   linguine
50 g ($^1/_2$ cup) freshly grated
   Parmesan cheese, to serve

➤ REMOVE MEMBRANE and seeds from the capsicum.

1 Slice into thin strips. Heat the oil in a large deep pan. Add the garlic and stir for 30 seconds over low heat.

2 Add the capsicum strips, tomatoes, zucchini, anchovies, capers, olives and 125 ml ($^1/_2$ cup) water to the pan. Cook for 20 minutes, stirring occasionally.

3 Stir in the basil, then season with salt and pepper. Meanwhile, add the pasta to a large saucepan of rapidly boiling water and cook until the pasta is just tender. Drain thoroughly. Divide pasta among warmed serving bowls and top with the sauce. Sprinkle with Parmesan and serve immediately.

COOK'S FILE

Storage time: Sauce can be made 1 day in advance.

1

2

3

TAGLIATELLE WITH SWEET TOMATO AND WALNUT SAUCE

Preparation time: 20 minutes
Total cooking time: 45 minutes
Serves 4–6

4 ripe tomatoes
1 medium carrot
1 tablespoon oil
1 onion, finely chopped
1 stick celery, finely chopped
2 tablespoons chopped fresh
    parsley
1 teaspoon red wine vinegar
60 ml (^{1}/4 cup) white wine
500 g (1 lb 2 oz) tagliatelle or
    fettuccine
1 tablespoon olive oil, extra
75 g (^{3}/4 cup) walnuts, roughly
    chopped
35 g (^{1}/3 cup) freshly grated
    Parmesan cheese, to serve

➤ MARK A SMALL CROSS on the bottom of each tomato.

1 Place the tomatoes in boiling water for 1–2 minutes, then plunge into cold water. Peel the skin down from the cross, then roughly chop the flesh. Grate the carrot.

2 Heat the oil in a large heavy-based pan and cook the onion and celery for 5 minutes over low heat, stirring regularly. Add the tomato, carrot, parsley and combined vinegar and wine. Reduce the heat and simmer for 25 minutes. Season to taste.

3 While the sauce is cooking, add the pasta to a large pan of rapidly boiling water and cook until just tender. Drain and return to the pan. Add sauce to pasta and toss to combine.

4 Five minutes before the sauce is cooked, heat the extra oil in a frying pan, add the walnuts and stir over low heat for 5 minutes. Serve the pasta and sauce topped with walnuts and sprinkled with Parmesan.

COOK'S FILE

Hints: It is handy to have fresh parsley on hand for use in cookery so try growing your own. You'll find it grows easily in the garden or in pots.

Pasta comes in different widths and thicknesses so choose whichever type you prefer.

The Italians often use Roma or egg tomatoes when cooking sauces so try them if they are available. You'll need about 6–8 as they are small.

SPAGHETTI AND MUSSELS IN TOMATO AND HERB SAUCE

Preparation time: 15 minutes
Total cooking time: 30 minutes
Serves 4

1 onion
1.5 kg (3 lb 5 oz) mussels in
    the shell
2 tablespoons olive oil
2 garlic cloves, crushed
425 g (15 oz) can tomatoes
250 ml (1 cup) white wine
1 tablespoon chopped fresh basil
2 tablespoons chopped fresh
    parsley
500 g (1 lb 2 oz) spaghetti

➤ PEEL ONION and slice finely.
1 Remove beards from the mussels and wash away any grit. Set aside.
2 Heat the oil in a large pan. Add the onion and garlic, and stir over low heat until the onion is tender. Add the crushed tomatoes, wine and herbs. Season with salt and pepper. Bring to the boil, reduce the heat, then simmer for 15–20 minutes, or until the sauce begins to thicken.

3 Add the mussels to the pan. Cook, covered, for about 5 minutes, shaking the pan occasionally. Discard any mussels that do not open during cooking. Meanwhile, add the spaghetti to a large pan of rapidly boiling water and cook until just tender. Drain immediately. Serve the mussels and sauce over the pasta.

COOK'S FILE

Hints: Serve with crusty bread and a crisp green salad.
    If fresh herbs are unavailable you can substitute with about one-third the amount of dried.

PASTA MARINARA

Preparation time: 10 minutes
Total cooking time: 20 minutes
Serves 4

250 g (9 oz) boneless fish fillets
1 large calamari (squid) tube
1 tablespoon olive oil
1 onion, sliced
1 garlic clove, crushed
125 ml ($^1/_2$ cup) red wine
2 tablespoons tomato paste
    (purée)
425 g (15 oz) can tomatoes
1 tablespoon chopped fresh
    basil
$^1/_4$ teaspoon dried oregano
150 g (5$^1/_2$ oz) medium raw
    prawns (shrimp), peeled and
    deveined (tails intact)
125 g (4$^1/_2$ oz) scallops, halved
125 g (4$^1/_2$ oz) mussel meat
    (optional)
500 g (1 lb 2 oz) linguine

➤ CUT FISH FILLETS into small even-sized pieces.
1 Thinly slice calamari. Heat the oil in a large frying pan. Add the onion and garlic; stir over low heat until onion is tender. Stir in the wine and tomato paste to combine. Simmer until the liquid is reduced by half. Stir in the crushed tomatoes.

2 Add the basil, oregano and season. Simmer gently for 10 minutes, stirring occasionally.
3 Add the fish, calamari, prawns, scallops and mussel meat to the sauce. Simmer, stirring, for 2–3 minutes, or until the flesh changes colour. Meanwhile, add the pasta to a large saucepan of rapidly boiling water and cook until just tender. Drain well. Serve the sauce over the pasta.

COOK'S FILE

Hints: Marinara mix is an economical method of preparing this dish and is readily available from fish shops.
    Overcooking of seafood will cause it to toughen.

Spaghetti and Mussels in Tomato and Herb Sauce (top) and
Pasta Marinara

LINGUINE WITH ANCHOVIES, OLIVES AND CAPERS

Preparation time: 15 minutes
Total cooking time: 20 minutes
Serves 4

500 g (1 lb 2 oz) linguine
2 tablespoons olive oil
2 garlic cloves, crushed
2 tomatoes, peeled and chopped (optional)
3 tablespoons capers
75 g (1/2 cup) chopped pitted black olives

55 g (1/4 cup) chopped pitted green olives
60 ml (1/4 cup) dry white wine
15 g (1/4 cup) chopped fresh parsley or basil
2 x 45 g (1 1/2 oz) cans anchovies, drained and chopped

➤ ADD LINGUINE to a large saucepan of rapidly boiling water and cook until just tender. Drain well. Return to the pan and keep warm.

1 Meanwhile, heat the oil in a frying pan. Add the garlic and stir over low heat for 1 minute. Add the tomato, capers and olives; cook for 2 minutes.

2 Stir in the wine and parsley, then season with pepper. Bring to the boil, then reduce the heat and simmer for 5 minutes. Remove pan from the heat.
3 Add the anchovies to the sauce, then add the sauce to the warm pasta. Gently toss together to distribute the sauce evenly through the pasta. Serve immediately.

COOK'S FILE

Hint: In a pan, heat a little olive oil and add some fresh breadcrumbs and a crushed clove of garlic; toss until crisp and golden. Sprinkle over pasta with Parmesan. This will add flavour and look attractive.

PASTA WITH CLAMS

Preparation time: 25 minutes
Total cooking time: 20 minutes
Serves 4

500 g (1 lb 2 oz) small shell
    pasta
1 kg (2 lb 4 oz) clams (vongole)
1 tablespoon olive oil
2 garlic cloves, crushed
2 x 425 g (15 oz) cans tomatoes
60 ml (1/4 cup) red wine
2 tablespoons chopped fresh
    parsley
1 teaspoon sugar

➤ HEAT A LARGE saucepan of water until water is boiling rapidly.

1 Add the pasta and cook until just tender. Drain and keep warm. Blend 2 tablespoons each of salt and plain (all-purpose) flour with enough water to make a paste. Add to a large pan of cold water and soak the shellfish in the mixture overnight. This will draw out the sand from inside the shells. Scrub the shells well. Rinse and drain.

2 Heat the oil in a large pan. Add the garlic and cook over low heat for 30 seconds. Add undrained, crushed tomatoes, wine, parsley, sugar, salt and freshly ground black pepper; stir. Bring to the boil, then reduce the heat and simmer, stirring occasionally, for 5 minutes.

3 Add scrubbed clams to pan. Cook over medium heat, stirring occasionally, until all shells have opened. Discard any that do not open. Divide pasta into warmed pasta bowls. Serve clams and sauce over pasta.

COOK'S FILE

Hints: If fresh clams are not available, use mussels, scallops or drained, tinned clams instead.

SPAGHETTI WITH CHILLI CALAMARI

Preparation time: 10 minutes
Total cooking time: 15 minutes
Serves 4

500 g (1 lb 2 oz) calamari
    (squid), cleaned
500 g (1 lb 2 oz) spaghetti
2 tablespoons olive oil
1 leek, chopped
2 garlic cloves, crushed
1–2 teaspoons chopped chilli
1/2 teaspoon cayenne pepper
425 g (15 oz) can tomatoes

125 ml (1/2 cup) fish stock
1 tablespoon chopped fresh basil
2 teaspoons chopped fresh sage
1 teaspoon chopped fresh
    marjoram

➤ PULL TENTACLES from body of calamari.

1 Using fingers pull quill from pouch of calamari. Pull skin away from flesh and discard. Using a sharp knife, slit the tubes up one side, lay out flat and score one side in a diamond pattern. Cut into four.

2 Add spaghetti to a large pan of rapidly boiling water and cook until just tender. Drain and keep warm.

Meanwhile, heat oil in a frying pan. Add leek and cook for 2 minutes. Stir in garlic for 1 minute over low heat, then chilli and cayenne. Add crushed tomatoes, stock and herbs. Bring to boil. Reduce heat; simmer 5 minutes.

3 Add calamari to pan. Simmer for another 5–10 minutes, or until tender. Serve Chilli Calamari over spaghetti. Serve with salad, if desired.

COOK'S FILE

Note: Prepare fish stock by covering fish bones and roughly chopped onion, celery and carrot with water. Bring to the boil. Reduce heat. Simmer for 30 minutes. Drain. Use immediately.

1

2

3

TAGLIATELLE WITH OCTOPUS

Preparation time: 15 minutes
Total cooking time: 20 minutes
Serves 4

500 g (1 lb 2 oz) mixed
  tagliatelle
1 kg (2 lb 4 oz) baby octopus
2 tablespoons olive oil
1 onion, sliced
1 garlic clove, crushed
425 g (15 oz) can puréed tomato
125 ml (½ cup) dry white wine

1 tablespoon chilli sauce
1 tablespoon chopped fresh
  basil

➤ ADD TAGLIATELLE to a large pan of rapidly boiling water and cook until just tender. Drain; keep warm.
1 Clean octopus (see Note) and cut them in half.
2 While pasta is cooking, heat oil in a large frying pan. Add onion and garlic and stir over low heat until onion is tender. Add puréed tomato, wine, chilli sauce and basil to pan. Season to taste. Bring to the boil. Reduce heat and simmer for 10 minutes.

3 Add octopus to pan. Simmer mixture for 5–10 minutes or until tender. Pour octopus sauce over pasta and serve immediately.

COOK'S FILE

Note: To clean octopus, use a small sharp knife and remove the gut by either cutting off the head entirely or by slicing open the head and removing the gut. Pick up the body and use the index finger to push beak up. Remove beak and discard. Clean octopus thoroughly. Cut sac into 2 or 3 pieces. Place cleaned octopus in a dish.

PAPPARDELLE WITH RABBIT AND CAPSICUM

Preparation time: 20 minutes
Total cooking time: 1 hour 50 minutes
Serves 4

60 ml (¼ cup) olive oil
1 rabbit, jointed (1 kg/2 lb 4 oz)
2 rashers rindless bacon, sliced
1 onion, sliced
2 stalks celery, chopped
1 garlic clove, crushed
2 tablespoons plain (all-purpose)
    flour
1 teaspoon dried marjoram
425 g (15 oz) can tomatoes
125 ml (½ cup) red wine
4 tablespoons tomato paste
    (purée)
1 capsicum (pepper), seeded
    and sliced
1 eggplant (aubergine),
    quartered and sliced
500 g (1 lb 2 oz) pappardelle
2 tablespoons freshly grated
    Parmesan cheese, for serving

➤ HEAT OIL in a large frying pan. Add the rabbit and brown well on all sides.

1 Transfer rabbit to a plate. Add bacon, onion, celery and garlic to the same pan. Stir over low heat until onion is soft.

2 Stir in flour and marjoram. Cook for 1 minute. Add crushed tomatoes, wine, tomato paste and 125 ml (½ cup) water; season and stir to combine.

3 Bring to the boil, stirring constantly. Reduce heat and return rabbit to pan. Simmer, covered, for 1½ hours, or until rabbit is very tender, adding more water as required. Remove rabbit from sauce. Allow to cool slightly. Remove flesh from bones, and discard the bones.

4 Return rabbit flesh to sauce with capsicum and eggplant. Simmer for another 15–20 minutes. About 15 minutes before sauce is ready, add pappardelle to a large pan of rapidly boiling water and cook until just tender. Drain well. Serve hot sauce over pasta. Sprinkle with a little Parmesan.

COOK'S FILE

Hint: Serve with crisp salad greens, or steamed carrots, beans or broccoli.

1

2

3

4

SPAGHETTI PIZZAIOLA

Preparation time: 15 minutes
Total cooking time: 30 minutes
Serves 4

2 tablespoons olive oil
2 garlic cloves, crushed
250 g (9 oz) minced (ground)
    beef or veal
2 x 425 g (15 oz) cans tomatoes
125 ml (1/2 cup) red wine
1 tablespoon chopped capers

1/2 teaspoon dried marjoram
1/2 teaspoon dried basil
2 tablespoons chopped fresh
    parsley
500 g (1 lb 2 oz) spaghetti

➤ HEAT OIL in a medium pan. Add garlic and stir over low heat for 1 minute.

1 Add meat and brown well, breaking up with a fork as it cooks.

2 Add to pan the undrained, crushed tomatoes, wine, capers, marjoram and basil. Season to taste. Bring to the boil. Reduce the heat and simmer, uncovered, for 20 minutes, or until the sauce is reduced by half. Add the parsley to the pan and stir to mix.

3 While the sauce is cooking, add the spaghetti to a large pan of rapidly boiling water and cook until it is just tender. Drain well and return to the pasta to the pan. Add the sauce to the pan and toss until mixed well. Serve immediately.

COOK'S FILE

Hint: Sprinkle with Parmesan cheese.

1

2

3

HOMESTYLE MEATBALLS WITH FUSILLI

Preparation time: 25 minutes
Total cooking time: 35 minutes
Serves 4

1 onion
750 g (1 lb 10 oz) minced (ground) pork and veal or beef
80 g (1 cup) fresh breadcrumbs
25 g (¼ cup) freshly grated Parmesan cheese
2 tablespoons chopped fresh parsley
1 egg, beaten
1 garlic clove, crushed
zest and juice of ½ lemon
30 g (¼ cup) plain (all-purpose) flour, seasoned
2 tablespoons olive oil
500 g (1 lb 2 oz) fusilli or spiral pasta

Sauce
425 g (15 oz) can puréed tomato
125 ml (½ cup) beef stock
125 ml (½ cup) red wine
2 tablespoons chopped fresh basil
1 garlic clove, crushed

► PEEL ONION and chop very finely.
1 In a large bowl, combine the meat, breadcrumbs, Parmesan, onion, parsley, egg, garlic and lemon zest and juice. Season with salt and pepper. Roll tablespoonsful of mixture into balls and roll balls in seasoned flour.
2 Place the oil in a large frying pan and fry the meatballs until golden. Remove from the pan and drain on paper towels. Set aside. Remove the excess fat and meat juices from the pan.
To make Sauce: In the same pan,

combine puréed tomato, stock, wine, basil and garlic. Season to taste with salt and pepper. Bring to the boil.
3 Reduce the heat and return the meatballs to pan. Allow to simmer for 10–15 minutes. Meanwhile, add fusilli to a large pan of rapidly boiling water

and cook until just tender. Drain well. Serve fusilli with meatballs and sauce over the top.

COOK'S FILE

Hint: If desired, add 1 sliced zucchini (courgette) to sauce in step 2.

1

2

3

GNOCCHI WITH TOMATO SAUCE

Preparation time: 35 minutes
Total cooking time: 45–50 minutes
Serves 4

500 g (1 lb 2 oz) potatoes, peeled and chopped
250 g (2 cups) plain (all-purpose) flour, sifted
25 g (^{1}/4 cup) freshly grated Parmesan cheese
30 g (1 oz) butter or margarine, melted
2 tablespoons freshly grated Parmesan cheese, plus extra, for serving

Tomato Sauce
1 kg (2 lb 4 oz) tomatoes, peeled and chopped
2 garlic cloves, crushed
125 ml (^{1}/2 cup) red wine
60 ml (^{1}/4 cup) finely chopped fresh basil

➤ COOK POTATO in pan of boiling water for 15–20 minutes or until soft.

1 Drain potato and mash until smooth. Transfer to a bowl. Add the flour, Parmesan, and butter. Season to taste with salt and pepper. Using a flat-bladed knife, mix to a firm dough. Knead on a lightly floured surface until smooth.

2 Roll heaped teaspoonsful of dough into oval shapes. Indent one side using the back of a fork. Cook in batches in a large pan of rapidly boiling water for 3–5 minutes each batch. Gnocchi will float when cooked. Drain well. Keep warm.

3 To make Tomato Sauce: In a pan, combine tomatoes, garlic, wine and basil. Season to taste. Bring to the boil. Reduce the heat and simmer for 15–20 minutes, or until sauce begins to thicken. Toss the gnocchi through sauce. Serve in warmed pasta bowls. Sprinkle with grated Parmesan cheese.

COOK'S FILE

Hint: For a meaty sauce, brown 250 g (9 oz) minced (ground) veal or beef in 1 tablespoon olive oil before adding Tomato Sauce ingredients.

1

2

3

RIGATONI WITH CHORIZO AND TOMATO

Preparation time: 15 minutes
Total cooking time: 20–25 minutes
Serves 4

1 onion
250 g (9 oz) chorizo sausage
2 tablespoons olive oil
425 g (15 oz) can tomatoes
125 ml (1/2 cup) dry white wine
1/2–1 teaspoon chopped chilli,
    optional

375 g (13 oz) rigatoni
2 tablespoons chopped fresh
    parsley, for serving
2 tablespoons freshly grated
    Parmesan cheese, for serving

➤ PEEL ONION and slice.
1 Cut the chorizo sausage into slices. Heat the oil in a large frying pan. Add the onion and stir over low heat until tender.
2 Add the sausage to the pan; cook, turning frequently, for 2–3 minutes. Add crushed tomatoes, wine and chilli. Season with salt and freshly ground

black pepper and stir. Bring to boil and reduce heat; simmer for 15–20 minutes.
3 Meanwhile, add the rigatoni to a large pan of rapidly boiling water and cook until just tender. Drain well and return to the pan. Add the sauce to the hot pasta with half of the combined parsley and Parmesan cheese. Toss to combine well. Serve sprinkled with remaining combined parsley and Parmesan cheese.

COOK'S FILE

Variation: Use different spicy sausage in place of chorizo.

1

2

3

ZITI WITH VEGETABLES AND SAUSAGE

Preparation time: 10 minutes
Total cooking time: 35 minutes
Serves 4

1 red capsicum (pepper)
1 green capsicum (pepper)
1 small eggplant (aubergine),
    sliced
60 ml ($^1/_4$ cup) olive oil
1 onion, sliced
1 garlic clove, crushed
250 g (9 oz) cocktail sausages,
    sliced
425 g (15 oz) can tomatoes
125 ml ($^1/_2$ cup) red wine
35 g ($^1/_4$ cup) halved pitted black
    olives
1 tablespoon chopped fresh basil
1 tablespoon chopped fresh
    parsley
500 g (1 lb 2 oz) ziti
2 tablespoons freshly grated
    Parmesan cheese, for serving

➤ CUT BOTH capsicum in half. Remove seeds and membrane.

1 Place capsicum under a hot grill. Cook until skin blackens and blisters. Cover with a damp tea towel. When cool, peel off skin. Chop and set aside.

2 Brush eggplant with a little oil. Grill until golden each side, brushing with more oil as required. Set aside.

3 Heat remaining oil in a frying pan. Add onion and garlic and stir over low heat until onion is tender. Add sausages and cook until well browned.

4 Stir in crushed tomatoes, wine, olives and herbs. Season with salt and freshly ground black pepper. Bring to the boil. Reduce heat and simmer for 15 minutes. Add vegetables and heat through. While sauce is cooking, add ziti to a large pan of rapidly boiling water until just tender. Drain well and return to pan. Toss vegetables and sauce through hot pasta. Sprinkle with Parmesan before serving.

COOK'S FILE

Hint: Serve with crisp green salad and crusty bread.

Ziti is a wide tubular pasta that is excellent with this dish but you can substitute fettuccine or spaghetti if you prefer.

1

2

3

4

PASTA WITH BRAISED OXTAIL AND CELERY

Preparation time: 20 minutes
Total cooking time: 3 hours 45 minutes
Serves 4

1.5 kg (3 lb 5 oz) oxtail, jointed
30 g ($^1/4$ cup) plain (all-purpose) flour, seasoned
60 ml ($^1/4$ cup) olive oil
1 onion, finely chopped
2 garlic cloves, crushed
500 ml (2 cups) beef stock
425 g (15 oz) can tomatoes
250 ml (1 cup) dry white wine
6 whole cloves

2 bay leaves
3 stalks celery, finely chopped
500 g (1 lb 2 oz) penne
30 g (1 oz) butter or margarine
25 g ($^1/4$ cup) freshly grated Parmesan cheese

➤ PREHEAT OVEN to 160°C (315°F/Gas 2–3).

1 Dust the oxtail in seasoned flour and shake off the excess. Heat half the oil in a large pan. Brown oxtail over high heat, a few pieces at a time. Transfer to a large casserole dish.

2 Wipe the pan clean with paper towels. Heat the remaining oil in the pan and add onion and garlic. Cook over low heat until the onion is tender. Stir in the stock, crushed tomatoes, wine, cloves and bay leaves. Season with salt and pepper. Bring to the boil. Pour over oxtail.

3 Bake, covered, for $2^1/2$–3 hours. Add celery to dish. Bake, uncovered, for another 30 minutes. Towards the end of cooking time, add pasta to a large pan of rapidly boiling water and cook until tender. Drain well. Toss with butter and Parmesan. Serve oxtail and sauce with pasta.

COOK'S FILE

Hint: Seasoned flour is plain flour to which seasonings of your choice have been added, for example, herbs, salt, pepper, dried mustard.

SPAGHETTI WITH SALAMI AND CAPSICUM

Preparation time: 15 minutes
Total cooking time: 55 minutes
Serves 4–6

2 tablespoons olive oil
1 large onion, finely chopped
2 garlic cloves, crushed
150 g (5½ oz) spicy salami
    slices, cut into strips
2 large red capsicum (peppers),
    chopped

825 g (1 lb 13 oz) can tomatoes
125 ml (½ cup) dry white wine
1 teaspoon dried basil
500 g (1 lb 2 oz) spaghetti

➤ HEAT OIL in a heavy-based frying pan.
1 Add onion, garlic and salami. Cook for 5 minutes, stirring, over medium heat. Add capsicum; cover pan and cook for 5 minutes.
2 Add undrained, crushed tomatoes, wine and basil. Bring to the boil and simmer, covered, for 15 minutes. Remove lid and cook for another

15 minutes, or until liquid is reduced and sauce is desired consistency. Season with salt and pepper.
3 Add pasta to a large pan of rapidly boiling water and cook until just tender; drain and return to pan. Toss half the sauce with the pasta; divide between warmed serving dishes; top with remaining sauce and serve.

COOK'S FILE

Hints: Salami should be chosen according to your taste. Use less spicy salami if you prefer.

Sprinkle with grated fresh parmesan.

1

2

3

PASTA SALADS

LINGUINE WITH BACON AND SESAME SEEDS

In a large salad bowl, combine 500 g (1 lb 2 oz) cooked, cooled linguine with 4 finely chopped rashers of crisp fried bacon, 3 finely chopped hard-boiled eggs, 50 g ($^1/2$ cup) freshly grated Parmesan cheese, 15 g ($^1/2$ cup) chopped fresh parsley and 40 g ($^1/4$ cup) toasted sesame seeds. Season, drizzle 60 ml ($^1/4$ cup) olive oil over the top and serve immediately. Garnish with fresh herbs, if desired. Serves 4–6.

Linguine with Bacon and Sesame Seeds

Spaghetti with Tomato and Olives

SPAGHETTI WITH TOMATO AND OLIVES

In a large salad bowl, combine 500 g (1 lb 2 oz) cooked, cooled spaghetti with 2 chopped tomatoes, 1 chopped red onion, 60 g ($^1/2$ cup) olives and 20 g (1 cup) fresh parsley leaves. Drizzle over dressing made by combining 60 ml ($^1/4$ cup) balsamic vinegar and 125 ml ($^1/2$ cup) olive oil; season, to taste, with salt and pepper. Serves 4–6.

PENNE WITH BROAD BEANS AND ARTICHOKES

In a large salad bowl, combine 500 g (1 lb 2 oz) cooked, cooled penne with 370 g (2 cups) blanched, peeled broad (fava) beans, 4 chopped spring onions (scallions), 6 quartered artichoke hearts, 45 g ($^1/2$ cup) grated pecorino cheese and 60 ml ($^1/4$ cup) olive oil. Season with salt and pepper. Garnish with fresh herbs, if desired. Serves 4–6.

FETTUCCINE WITH CHICKEN AND WALNUTS

In a large salad bowl, combine 500 g (1 lb 2 oz) cooked, cooled fettuccine with 350 g (2 cups) cooked, shredded chicken, 50 g ($^1/2$ cup) toasted walnuts, 60 g ($^1/2$ cup) olives, 30 g (1 cup) fresh basil leaves and 60 ml ($^1/4$ cup) lemon juice. Season, toss and serve immediately. Serves 4–6.

Penne with Broad Beans and Artichokes

Fettuccine with Chicken and Walnuts

*Farfalle with
Tuna and Capers*

*Tagliatelle, Rocket and
Sundried Tomatoes*

TAGLIATELLE, ROCKET AND SUNDRIED TOMATOES

In a salad bowl, combine 500 g (1 lb 2 oz) cooked, cooled tagliatelle with 105 g (3 cups) rocket (arugula) leaves, 10 chopped sundried (sun-blushed) tomatoes, 1 avocado, cut into slices, and a dressing of 125 ml ($^1/_2$ cup) olive oil, 60 ml ($^1/_4$ cup) white wine vinegar, and 1 tablespoon seeded mustard. Toss well and season. Serves 4–6.

MACARONI WITH SPINACH AND BACON

In a salad bowl, combine 500 g (1 lb 2 oz) cooked macaroni, 130 g (2 cups) shredded spinach, 4 slices crisp cooked bacon and a few slices of chopped prosciutto, 1 chopped red onion and 25 g ($^1/_4$ cup) freshly grated Parmesan cheese. Drizzle 125 ml ($^1/_2$ cup) olive oil over the top and season to taste. Toss well and serve. Serves 4–6.

*Spiral Pasta and
Artichokes*

FARFALLE WITH TUNA AND CAPERS

In a salad bowl, combine 500 g (1 lb 2 oz) cooked, cooled farfalle (butterfly pasta) with 425 g (15 oz) can drained, flaked tuna, 200 g (7 oz) chopped mozzarella cheese, 60 g ($^1/_2$ cup) black olives, 6 tablespoons drained capers, fried in 1 tablespoon oil until crisp, and 15 g ($^1/_2$ cup) chopped fresh basil. Toss well with 125 ml ($^1/_2$ cup) lemon juice. Season. Garnish with strips of lemon rind, if desired. Serves 4–6.

SPIRAL PASTA AND ARTICHOKES

Arrange some butter lettuce leaves on a platter, top with 500 g (1 lb 2 oz) cooked, cooled spiral pasta, 10 quartered artichoke hearts and 8 slices crisp cooked chopped pancetta. Toss with a dressing of 2 chopped garlic cloves, 60 ml ($^1/_4$ cup) lemon juice, 125 ml ($^1/_2$ cup) olive oil. Season. Serves 4–6.

59

*Macaroni with Spinach
and Bacon*

CREAMY PASTA

TAGLIATELLE WITH ASPARAGUS AND HERBS

Preparation time: 15 minutes
Total cooking time: 15 minutes
Serves 4–6

500 g (1 lb 2 oz) tagliatelle
1 bunch asparagus
40 g (1¹/2 oz) butter
1 tablespoon chopped fresh
  parsley
1 tablespoon chopped fresh
  basil
300 ml (1¹/4 cups) cream
50 g (¹/2 cup) freshly grated
  Parmesan cheese

► COOK PASTA in a large pan of rapidly boiling water and cook until just tender. Drain and return to pan.

1 While the pasta is cooking, cut asparagus spears into short pieces.
2 Heat the butter in a medium pan, stir asparagus, over medium heat, for 2 minutes, or until just tender.
3 Add the chopped parsley and basil, and cream. Season to taste with salt and freshly ground black pepper. Cook for 2 minutes.
4 Add the grated Parmesan cheese to the pan and stir well. When thoroughly mixed, add to the warm pasta in the pan and toss gently to distribute the ingredients evenly. Serve in warmed pasta bowls.

COOK'S FILE

Hints: This dish looks attractive if you shave some extra Parmesan cheese and use it for garnish.

If desired, you can serve this dish as a first course for 8 people.

SPAGHETTI CARBONARA

Preparation time: 10 minutes
Total cooking time: 25 minutes
Serves 4–6

8 rashers bacon
500 g (1 lb 2 oz) spaghetti
4 eggs
50 g (1/2 cup) freshly grated
   Parmesan cheese
300 ml (1 1/4 cups) cream

➤ REMOVE RIND from the bacon and discard. Cut the bacon into thin strips.

1 Add the bacon strips to a heavy-based frying pan and cook over medium heat until crisp. Remove and drain on paper towels.

2 Add pasta to a large pan of rapidly boiling water and cook until just just tender. Drain in a colander and return to pan. Set aside.

3 While pasta is cooking, beat eggs, parmesan and cream in a small bowl. Add bacon to bowl and pour mixture over the hot pasta; toss well. Return pan to heat and cook mixture, over very low heat, for 1/2–1 minute, or until mixture just thickens. Add the pepper and serve immediately. May be garnished with sprigs of fresh herbs, if desired.

COOK'S FILE

Storage time: Best cooked just before serving.

Hint: Take care not to overcook sauce as it can curdle. Make sure the heat is very low after you have combined pasta with sauce. If you are using an electric element you can turn the heat off at this stage.

1

2

3

FETTUCCINE ALFREDO

Preparation time: 10 minutes
Total cooking time: 15 minutes
Serves 4–6

500 g (1 lb 2 oz) fettuccine
100 g (3¹/2 oz) butter
150 g (1¹/2 cups) freshly grated
  Parmesan cheese

300 ml (1¹/4 cups) cream
15 g (¹/4 cup) chopped fresh
  parsley

➤ ADD PASTA to a large pan of rapidly boiling water and cook until just tender. Drain in a colander and return to the pan.

1 While the pasta is cooking, heat the butter in a medium pan over low heat. Add the Parmesan and cream, bring to the boil and stir regularly.

2 Add the parsley, season to taste with salt and freshly ground black pepper and stir to combine.

3 Add the sauce to the pasta and toss well. Serve immediately.

COOK'S FILE

Hints: This dish will serve 8 as a first course.

Garnish with grated Parmesan.

PENNE WITH CREAMY TOMATO SAUCE

Preparation time: 25 minutes
Total cooking time: 20 minutes
Serves 4–6

2 rashers bacon
4 large ripe tomatoes
500 g (1 lb 2 oz) penne
1 tablespoon olive oil
2 spring onions (scallions), chopped
2 tablespoons chopped fresh basil
300 ml (1¼ cups) cream

➤ REMOVE AND DISCARD bacon rind. Cut bacon into small pieces.

1 Using a sharp knife, mark a small cross on the bottom of each tomato. Place the tomatoes in boiling water for 1–2 minutes, then plunge into cold water. Remove from the water and peel the skin down from cross.

2 Cut the tomatoes in half and scoop out the seeds with a teaspoon. Finely chop the flesh. Add pasta to a large pan of rapidly boiling water and cook until just tender. Drain; keep warm.

3 While pasta is cooking, heat oil in a heavy-based frying pan. Cook bacon and spring onion over medium heat, stirring occasionally, for 5 minutes. Add the basil and cream. Season with salt and freshly ground black pepper, and simmer for 5 minutes. Add the tomato and cook for 2–3 minutes, or until heated through. Divide pasta into warmed serving bowls. Top with sauce. Serve immediately.

COOK'S FILE

Storage time: If you like, you can prepare the tomatoes the day before cooking the dish and store in a sealed container in refrigerator.

SPAGHETTI WITH GORGONZOLA SAUCE

Preparation time: 10 minutes
Total cooking time: 20 minutes
Serves 4–6

375 g (13 oz) spaghetti or
   bucatini
200 g (7 oz) gorgonzola cheese
20 g (1/2 oz) butter

1 stick celery, finely chopped
300 ml (1 1/4 cups) cream
250 g (9 oz) fresh ricotta cheese,
   beaten until smooth

➤ ADD PASTA to a large pan of rapidly boiling water and cook until just tender. Drain and return to pan.

1 While the pasta is cooking, chop gorgonzola cheese into small cubes.

2 Heat butter in a medium frying pan, add celery and stir for 2 minutes.

Add the cream, ricotta and gorgonzola cheeses. Season to taste with salt and freshly ground black pepper.

3 Bring to boil over low heat, stirring constantly, simmer 1 minute. Add sauce to pasta and toss well to combine.

COOK'S FILE

Hint: Garnish with chopped fresh parsley, if desired.

Note: Gorgonzola is a rich, strong Italian blue-veined cheese.

1

2

3

SHELLS WITH BROCCOLI AND ANCHOVY

Preparation time: 15 minutes
Total cooking time: 20 minutes
Serves 4–6

500 g (1 lb 2 oz) small shell pasta
450 g (1 lb) broccoli
1 tablespoon olive oil
1 onion, chopped
1 garlic clove, crushed
3 anchovy fillets, chopped
300 ml (1¼ cups) cream
50 g (½ cup) freshly grated
    Parmesan cheese, for serving

➤ ADD PASTA to a large pan of boiling water and cook until just tender. Drain and return to pan.

1 While the pasta is cooking, cut the broccoli into small florets. Cook the broccoli in a pan of boiling water for 1 minute, then drain. Place in cold water and drain again. Set aside.

2 Heat oil in a heavy-based frying pan. Add the chopped onion, crushed garlic and chopped anchovies and cook over low heat, stirring, for 3 minutes.

3 Add the cream to the pan and, stirring constantly, bring to the boil. Reduce the heat and simmer for 2 minutes. Add the broccoli florets and cook for 1 minute. Season with salt and freshly ground black pepper. Add the sauce to the pasta and toss well to combine. Serve in warmed pasta plates. Sprinkle with freshly grated Parmesan cheese and serve immediately.

COOK'S FILE

Hints: When tossing sauce with the pasta, make sure all pieces of pasta are thoroughly coated with sauce. You can substitute different pastas such as macaroni or farfalle (butterfly pasta) if you prefer.
Variation: Use freshly grated pecorino cheese instead of Parmesan.

1

2

3

SPINACH FETTUCCINE WITH MUSHROOM SAUCE

Preparation time: 15 minutes
Total cooking time: 25 minutes
Serves 4–6

500 g (1 lb 2 oz) spinach or
    plain fettuccine
300 g (10½ oz) baby mushrooms
3 spring onions (scallions)
6 slices smoked ham or
    pancetta (50 g/1¾ oz)
40 g (1½ oz) butter
2 tablespoons chopped fresh
    parsley

300 ml (1¼ cups) cream
2 tablespoons chopped fresh
    parsley, extra, for serving

➤ ADD PASTA to a large pan of rapidly boiling water and cook until just tender. Drain and return to pan.

1 Meanwhile, slice the mushrooms finely. Trim the spring onions, removing the dark green section, then chop finely. Slice the smoked ham or pancetta into thin strips.

2 Heat the butter in a pan, cook spring onion and ham over medium heat for 3 minutes. Add mushrooms to pan. Cover pan and reduce heat; cook, stirring occasionally, for 5 minutes.

3 Add parsley and cream. Season to taste with salt and freshly ground black pepper, then simmer for 2 minutes. Add sauce to pasta and toss well to combine. Serve immediately in warmed pasta bowls. Sprinkle with extra parsley.

COOK'S FILE

Hints: Don't add all the pasta to the boiling water at once—add it gradually, making sure that the water continues to boil.

If spinach fettuccine is unavailable, you can use other varieties of pasta. Dried or fresh pasta are both delicious with this sauce.

1

2

3

Shells with Broccoli and Anchovy (top) and
Spinach Fettuccine with Mushroom Sauce

RIGATONI WITH PUMPKIN SAUCE

Preparation time: 15 minutes
Total cooking time: 25 minutes
Serves 4–6

1 kg (2 lb 4 oz) pumpkin
2 medium leeks
40 g (1½ oz) butter
½ teaspoon ground nutmeg
500 g (1 lb 2 oz) rigatoni or
 large penne
300 ml (1¼ cups) cream
40 g (¼ cup) toasted pine
 nuts

➤ PEEL PUMPKIN, discard seeds and cut pumpkin into small cubes.

1 Remove and discard outer leaves and dark green section of leeks. Wash leeks thoroughly to remove all grit. Using a sharp knife, slice leeks finely.

2 Heat butter in large pan over low heat. Add sliced leek, cover pan and cook, stirring occasionally, for 5 minutes. Add pumpkin and nutmeg, cover and cook for 8 minutes. While vegetables are cooking, add pasta to a large pan of boiling water and cook until just tender. Drain and keep warm.

3 Add cream and 60 ml (¼ cup) water to pumpkin; bring sauce to the boil. Cook, stirring occasionally, for

8 minutes, or until pumpkin is tender. Divide pasta between warmed serving bowls and top with sauce. Sprinkle with pine nuts and serve immediately.

COOK'S FILE

Hints: Butternut (squash) or Japanese pumpkin will give the sweetest flavour to this sauce.

To toast pine nuts, stir over low heat in a non-stick frying pan until lightly golden. Alternatively, spread on a baking tray and grill—be sure to check frequently as they brown quickly.

Variations: Add more nutmeg if you like a stronger flavour.

Use a smaller pasta, if preferred.

SPIRALS WITH BROAD BEAN SAUCE

Preparation time: 30 minutes
Total cooking time: 25 minutes
Serves 4–6

500 g (1 lb 2 oz) spiral pasta or
    penne
310 g (2 cups) frozen broad
    (fava) beans
4 rashers bacon
2 medium leeks
2 tablespoons olive oil
300 ml (1$^1/_4$ cups) cream
2 teaspoons grated lemon zest

➤ ADD PASTA to a large pan of rapidly boiling water and cook until just tender. Drain and return to pan.

1 While pasta is cooking, plunge broad beans into a medium pan of boiling water. Remove immediately and cool in cold water. Drain and allow to cool. Peel rough outside skin from beans.

2 Remove and discard rind from bacon. Chop bacon into small pieces. Remove and discard outer leaves and dark green section of leeks. Wash leeks thoroughly to remove all dirt and grit. Using a sharp knife, slice leeks finely.

3 Heat oil in a heavy-based frying pan. Add leek and bacon and cook over medium heat, stirring occasionally, for 8 minutes or until leek is golden. Add cream and lemon zest; cook for 2 minutes. Add prepared broad beans, then season with salt and pepper.

4 Add sauce to pasta and toss well to combine. Serve immediately in warmed pasta bowls.

COOK'S FILE

Storage time: Broad beans can be cooked and peeled in advance and refrigerated in a covered container.

Hint: To peel broad beans, break the top off and squeeze beans out. Leaving the hard outside skin on the broad bean will change the delicate texture and flavour of this dish—peeling is worth the extra effort.

Fresh broad beans can be used instead of frozen. If they are very young, you can leave the skin on. Old beans must be peeled. Cook, after peeling, 15 minutes and add to dish.

1

2

3

4

SPAGHETTI WITH PRIMAVERA SAUCE

Preparation time: 25 minutes
Total cooking time: 15 minutes
Serves 4–6

500 g (1 lb 2 oz) spaghetti or
    fettuccine
1 bunch fresh asparagus
155 g (1 cup) frozen broad (fava)
    beans
40 g (1¹⁄₂ oz) butter
1 stick celery, sliced
155 g (1 cup) frozen peas
300 ml (1¹⁄₄ cups) cream
50 g (¹⁄₂ cup) freshly grated
    Parmesan cheese

➤ ADD PASTA to a pan of rapidly boiling water and cook until just tender. Drain and return to pan.

1 While pasta is cooking, cut asparagus into small pieces. Bring a medium pan of water to the boil, add asparagus, cook 2 minutes. Using a slotted spoon, remove from pan and plunge in cold water.

2 Plunge broad beans into a medium pan of boiling water. Remove immediately and cool in cold water. Drain and allow to cool. Peel rough outside skin from broad beans.

3 Heat butter in a heavy-based frying pan. Add celery and stir for 2 minutes. Add peas and cream; cook for 3 minutes. Add asparagus, broad beans and Parmesan. Season and bring to the boil; cook for 1 minute. Add sauce to spaghetti and toss to combine. Serve immediately in warmed pasta bowls.

COOK'S FILE

Variation: Use different vegetables such as leeks, zucchini (courgette) and sugar peas with fresh chopped dill or basil.

SPAGHETTI WITH CREAMY GARLIC MUSSELS

Preparation time: 20 minutes
Total cooking time: 12 minutes
Serves 4

500 g (1 lb 2 oz) spaghetti
1.5 kg (3 lb 5 oz) mussels in the shell
2 tablespoons olive oil
2 garlic cloves, crushed
125 ml (¹/2 cup) white wine
250 ml (1 cup) cream
2 tablespoons chopped fresh basil

➤ ADD SPAGHETTI to a large saucepan of rapidly boiling water and cook until just tender. Drain and keep the pasta warm.

1 While the spaghetti is cooking, remove the beards from mussels and wash away any grit. Set aside. Heat the oil in a large pan. Add garlic and stir over low heat for 30 seconds.

2 Add the wine and mussels. Simmer, covered, for 5 minutes. Remove mussels and set aside.

3 Add the cream and basil to the pan. Season to taste with salt and freshly ground black pepper. Simmer for 2 minutes, stirring occasionally. Serve sauce and mussels over spaghetti.

COOK'S FILE

Hint: Serve with crusty bread.

1

2

3

CREAMY PRAWNS WITH FETTUCCINE

Preparation time: 20 minutes
Total cooking time: 15 minutes
Serves 4

500 g (1 lb 2 oz) fettuccine
500 g (1 lb 2 oz) raw prawns
   (shrimp)
30 g (1 oz) butter or margarine
1 tablespoon olive oil
6 spring onions (scallions),
   chopped
1 garlic clove, crushed
250 ml (1 cup) cream
2 tablespoons chopped fresh
   parsley, for serving

➤ ADD FETTUCCINE to a large pan of rapidly boiling water and cook until just tender. Drain well; return to pan.

1 While fettuccine is cooking, peel and devein prawns.

2 Heat butter and oil in a frying pan. Add spring onion and garlic and stir over low heat 1 minute. Add prawns. Cook for 2–3 minutes, or until flesh changes colour. Remove the prawns from pan and set aside. Add cream to pan and bring to the boil. Reduce heat and simmer until sauce begins to thicken. Return the prawns to the pan; season to taste with salt and pepper. Simmer for 1 minute.

3 Add the prawns and sauce to the fettuccine and toss. Serve in warmed pasta bowls. Sprinkle with parsley.

COOK'S FILE

Variations: In step 1, add 1 red capsicum (pepper), seeded and sliced, and 1 leek, dark green section removed and white part cleaned thoroughly and sliced very finely.

Use scallops instead of prawns or a mixture of both.

1

2

3

FARFALLE WITH TUNA, MUSHROOMS AND CREAM

Preparation time: 10 minutes
Total cooking time: 15 minutes
Serves 4

60 g (2¼ oz) butter or
    margarine
1 tablespoon olive oil
1 onion, chopped
1 garlic clove, crushed
125 g (4½ oz) mushrooms,
    sliced

250 ml (1 cup) cream
450 g (1 lb) can tuna, drained
    and flaked
1 tablespoon lemon juice
1 tablespoon chopped fresh
    parsley
500 g (1 lb 2 oz) farfalle
    (butterfly pasta)

➤ HEAT BUTTER and oil in large frying pan. Add onion and garlic; stir over low heat until onion is tender.

1 Add mushrooms to pan. Cook for 2 minutes. Pour in cream. Bring to the boil. Reduce heat. Simmer until sauce begins to thicken.

2 Add flaked tuna, lemon juice and parsley to cream mixture; season with salt and pepper and stir to combine. Heat gently, stirring constantly.

3 While sauce is cooking, add farfalle to a large pan of rapidly boiling water and cook until just tender. Drain well and return to pan. Add sauce to farfalle and toss to combine. Serve in warmed pasta bowls.

COOK'S FILE

Hint: Serve with a fresh green salad or steamed vegetables.

Variation: Use a can of salmon, drained and flaked, instead of tuna.

FETTUCCINE WITH SMOKED SALMON

Preparation time: 10 minutes
Total cooking time: 10 minutes
Serves 4

100 g (3½ oz) smoked salmon
35 g (¼ cup) sundried
    (sun-blushed) tomatoes
1 tablespoon olive oil
1 garlic clove, crushed
250 ml (1 cup) cream
¼ teaspoon mustard powder

15 g (¼ cup) snipped fresh
    chives
2 teaspoons lemon juice
375 g (13 oz) fettuccine
2 tablespoons freshly grated
    Parmesan, for serving
snipped fresh chives, extra, for
    serving

➤ SLICE SMOKED salmon into pieces.
1 Chop sundried tomatoes. Heat oil in a frying pan. Add garlic and stir over low heat for 30 seconds. Add cream, mustard powder and chives. Season to taste with salt and freshly ground black pepper; bring to the boil. Reduce heat and simmer, stirring, until sauce begins to thicken.
2 Add salmon and lemon juice; stir to combine. Heat gently. Meanwhile, add the pasta to large pan of rapidly boiling water; cook until just tender. Drain well and return to pan.
3 Toss sauce through hot pasta. Serve immediately topped with sundried tomatoes, Parmesan and chives.

COOK'S FILE

Hint: Grow your own chives in the garden or in pots.

1

2

3

FETTUCCINE WITH CAVIAR

Preparation time: 15 minutes
Total cooking time: 15 minutes
Serves 4

2 hard-boiled eggs
4 spring onions (scallions)
250 g (1 cup) light sour cream
50 g (1¾ oz) red caviar
2 tablespoons chopped fresh dill

1 tablespoon lemon juice
500 g (1 lb 2 oz) fettuccine

➤ PEEL EGGS and chop into small pieces. Trim the spring onions, discarding dark green tops; chop finely.

1 In a small bowl place the sour cream, chopped eggs, spring onion, caviar, dill, lemon juice and freshly ground black pepper, to taste. Mix ingredients well and set aside.

2 Add the fettuccine to a large saucepan of rapidly boiling water and cook until just tender. Drain well, then return to the pan.

3 Toss the caviar mixture through the hot pasta. Serve garnished with a sprig of fresh dill, if desired.

COOK'S FILE

Note: Use large red roe, not small supermarket variety.
Hint: To hard-boil an egg, place cold egg in cold water. Bring water to the boil, simmer 5–6 minutes. Cool under cold running water.

PENNE WITH CHICKEN AND MUSHROOMS

Preparation time: 15 minutes
Total cooking time: 25 minutes
Serves 4

30 g (1 oz) butter or margarine
1 tablespoon olive oil
1 onion, sliced
1 garlic clove, crushed
60 g (2¹/4 oz) prosciutto,
 chopped
250 g (9 oz) chicken thigh
 fillets, trimmed and sliced
125 g (4¹/2 oz) mushrooms,
 sliced

1 tomato, peeled, halved and
 sliced
1 tablespoon tomato paste
 (purée)
125 ml (¹/2 cup) white wine
250 ml (1 cup) cream
500 g (1 lb 2 oz) penne
2 tablespoons freshly grated
 Parmesan cheese, for serving

➤ HEAT BUTTER and oil in a large frying pan.

1 Add onion and garlic and stir over low heat until onion is tender. Add prosciutto to pan and fry until crisp.

2 Add chicken and cook over medium heat for 3 minutes. Add mushrooms and cook for another 2 minutes.

Add tomato and tomato paste and stir until combined. Add wine and stir. Bring to the boil. Reduce heat and simmer until liquid is reduced by half.

3 Stir in cream, salt and pepper. Bring to the boil. Reduce heat and simmer until sauce begins to thicken. While sauce is cooking, add penne to a large pan of rapidly boiling water and cook until just tender. Drain well and return to pan. Add sauce to pasta and toss to combine. Serve immediately, sprinkled with Parmesan.

COOK'S FILE

Hint: If you prefer, you can use minced (ground) chicken in this recipe instead of sliced chicken fillets.

RIGATONI WITH SAUSAGE AND PARMESAN

Preparation time: 10 minutes
Total cooking time: 15 minutes
Serves 4

60 g (2¹/4 oz) mushrooms, sliced
500 g (1 lb 2 oz) Italian pork
 sausage or salami
2 tablespoons olive oil
1 onion, sliced
1 garlic clove, crushed
125 ml (¹/2 cup) dry white wine
500 g (1 lb 2 oz) rigatoni

250 ml (1 cup) cream
2 eggs
50 g (¹/2 cup) freshly grated
 Parmesan cheese
2 tablespoons chopped fresh
 parsley

➤ SLICE MUSHROOMS finely.

1 Cut the sausage into bite-sized chunks. Heat the oil in a large frying pan.

2 Add the onion and garlic and stir over low heat until the onion is tender. Add the sausage and mushrooms. Cook until sausage is cooked through. Add the wine and bring the mixture to

the boil. Reduce the heat and simmer until reduced by half.

3 While the sauce is cooking, add rigatoni to a large saucepan of rapidly boiling water and cook until just tender. Drain well, then return to the pan. In a large jug, whisk together the cream, eggs, 25 g (¹/4 cup) of the Parmesan and the parsley. Season with salt and pepper. Add to rigatoni; add sausage mixture; toss. Serve sprinkled with remaining Parmesan.

COOK'S FILE

Hint: You can freeze leftover wine for use in recipes such as this one.

Penne with Chicken and Mushrooms (top) and
Rigatoni with Sausage and Parmesan

TAGLIATELLE WITH CHICKEN LIVERS AND CREAM

Preparation time: 20 minutes
Total cooking time: 15 minutes
Serves 4

1 onion
300 g (10 1/2 oz) chicken livers
2 tablespoons olive oil
1 garlic clove, crushed
250 ml (1 cup) cream
1 tablespoon snipped chives
1 teaspoon seeded mustard

2 eggs, beaten
375 g (13 oz) tagliatelle
2 tablespoons freshly grated
Parmesan cheese, for serving
snipped chives, for serving

► PEEL ONION and chop finely.
1 Trim the chicken livers and chop them into small pieces.
2 Heat the oil in a large frying pan. Add the onion and garlic and stir over low heat until the onion is tender. Add the chicken livers to pan, then cook gently for 2–3 minutes. Remove from the heat. Stir the cream, chives and seeded mustard into the chicken livers. Season to taste with salt and freshly ground black pepper. Return the pan to the heat. Bring to the boil.
3 Add the beaten eggs and stir quickly to combine. Remove the pan from the heat. Meanwhile, add the tagliatelle to a large pan of rapidly boiling water and cook until just tender. Drain well and return to pan. Add sauce to hot pasta and toss well to combine. Serve in warmed pasta bowls. Sprinkle with the Parmesan cheese and snipped chives.

COOK'S FILE

Hint: Snip chives with kitchen scissors.

LINGUINE WITH LEMON CREAMY SAUCE

Preparation time: 10 minutes
Total cooking time: 20 minutes
Serves 4

400 g (14 oz) fresh linguine or
   spaghetti
300 ml (1$^{1}/_{4}$ cups) cream
250 ml (1 cup) chicken stock

1 tablespoon grated lemon zest
$^{1}/_{4}$ teaspoon saffron threads or
   powder (optional)

➤ ADD PASTA to a large pan of rapidly boiling water until just tender. Drain and keep warm.

1 While pasta is cooking, combine cream, chicken stock and lemon zest in a large frying pan. Bring to the boil, stirring occasionally.

2 Reduce heat and simmer for 10 minutes. Season to taste with salt and freshly ground black pepper. Add cooked pasta and cook for another 2–3 minutes.

3 Sprinkle with saffron threads; stir and serve immediately. Garnish with fine strips of lemon rind, if desired.

COOK'S FILE

Hint: Saffron is available from delicatessens and specialty food shops. If unavailable, use $^{1}/_{4}$ teaspoon turmeric.

SEMOLINA GNOCCHI BAKED WITH CHEESE

Preheat oven to 180°C (350°F/Gas 4). Grease a 1.5 litre (6 cup) ovenproof dish. Bring 1 litre (4 cups) milk to the boil in a pan. Slowly sprinkle 250 g (9 oz) fine semolina over the surface of the milk, whisking to prevent lumps. Cook for 5–8 minutes stirring constantly until mixture forms a smooth thick ball. Stir in 2 egg yolks, 50 g (1/2 cup) freshly grated Parmesan cheese, 125 ml (1/2 cup) melted butter and season. Lightly dampen bench top with water, spread semolina mixture onto surface with a wet flat-bladed knife. Smooth out mixture to about 1 cm (1/2 inch) thick. Cut into rounds with a wet 6 cm (21/2 inch) cutter. Place half of gnocchi rounds in the base of the dish; pour over 170 ml (2/3 cup) puréed tomato and place remaining gnocchi rounds over the top. Sprinkle with 50 g (1/2 cup) freshly grated Parmesan cheese and dot with butter. Bake 20–25 minutes, or until crisp and golden brown. Garnish with fresh basil leaves. Serves 4–6.

Spinach and Ricotta Gnocchi

GNOCCHI

SPINACH AND RICOTTA GNOCCHI

Place 4 slices crustless white bread in a shallow dish. Cover with 125 ml (1/2 cup) milk and allow to stand for 10 minutes. Squeeze out excess liquid. Thaw 500 g (1 lb 2 oz) frozen spinach and squeeze out all excess liquid. Place bread, spinach, 250 g (9 oz) ricotta cheese, 3 eggs, 50 g (1/2 cup) freshly grated Parmesan cheese, 1/2 teaspoon nutmeg, and salt and pepper, in a food processor. Process for 20 seconds, or until combined. Chill for 1 hour. Lightly coat your fingertips in flour and roll rounded teaspoonsful of mixture into little flat dumplings. Bring a pan of water to a gentle boil, cook 5 gnocchi at a time for about 2 minutes, or until they float; transfer to warmed serving plates with a slotted spoon. Serve immediately, drizzled with foaming butter. Garnish with shaved Parmesan cheese and sage leaves, if desired. Serves 4–6 .

NOTE: Spinach gnocchi is very soft and must be handled gently—not over-handled or it will toughen and break up.

Semolina Gnocchi Baked with Cheese

DRY-ROASTED PUMPKIN GNOCCHI WITH NUTMEG

Cut 1.5 kg (3 lb 5 oz) butternut pumpkin (squash) into large wedges, place in a baking dish and cook for 1 hour, or until tender. Cool and peel. Process in a food processor until smooth. Place in a bowl. Stir in 250 g (2 cups) plain (all-purpose) flour, 2 tablespoons freshly grated Parmesan cheese and 1 egg. Cover and refrigerate $1^1/2$ hours. Preheat oven to 180°C (350°F/Gas 4). Fit a large piping bag with a star nozzle and fill with mixture. Hold the piping bag over the boiling water; squeeze the mixture out and cut into lengths using scissors, letting gnocchi fall into the water. Cook in 4 batches for about 4 minutes, or until they float. Transfer to warmed serving dishes with a slotted spoon. Serve immediately with foaming butter, sprinkled with freshly ground nutmeg. Garnish with sprigs of fresh oregano, if desired. Serves 4–6.

Potato Gnocchi with Tomato and Basil Sauce

Dry-roasted Pumpkin Gnocchi with Nutmeg

POTATO GNOCCHI WITH TOMATO AND BASIL SAUCE

Heat 1 tablespoon oil in a frying pan. Add 1 chopped onion, 1 stick chopped celery and 2 chopped carrots. Cook for 5 minutes, stirring regularly. Add 825 g (1 lb 13 oz) can crushed tomatoes with liquid and 1 teaspoon sugar. Season. Bring to the boil, reduce heat and simmer over very low heat 20 minutes. Process in a food processor until smooth; add 30 g ($1/2$ cup) chopped fresh basil leaves. Set aside. Peel and chop 1 kg (2 lb 4 oz) potatoes; cook 15 minutes in boiling water until very tender. Drain and mash until smooth. Stir in 30 g (1 oz) butter and 250 g (2 cups) plain (all-purpose) flour. Beat in 2 eggs. Cool. Turn potato mixture onto a floured surface, divide into 2, roll each batch into long sausages. Cut into 3–4 cm ($1^1/4$–$1^1/2$ inch) pieces; roll each piece along the outside of a fork to give traditional pattern. Cook gnocchi in 4 batches in boiling water for about 3 minutes, or until they float. Transfer to warmed serving plates with a slotted spoon. Serve with tomato sauce and Parmesan cheese. Serves 4–6.

NOTE: Gnocchi must not be handled more than necessary or overcooked or it becomes tough. Keep all ingredients chilled and the kitchen cool.

Gnocchi can be made and formed into desired shapes before freezing in between freezer paper in an airtight container. It will keep for up to 2 months. When you wish to use it, cook frozen (do not defrost) in boiling water, adding 30 seconds extra cooking time if necessary.

BAKED & FILLED

BASIL TORTELLINI WITH BACON AND TOMATO SAUCE

Preparation: 15 minutes
Total cooking time: 25 minutes
Serves 4

500 g (1 lb 2 oz) fresh or
    dried basil tortellini or
    orecchiette
1 tablespoon olive oil
4 rashers bacon, chopped
2 garlic cloves, crushed
1 onion, chopped
1 teaspoon chopped fresh
    chillies
425 g (15 oz) can tomatoes
125 ml (½ cup) cream
2 tablespoons chopped fresh basil

➤ COOK PASTA in a pan of rapidly boiling water until just tender. Drain and return to pan.

1 While pasta is cooking, heat oil in a medium heavy-based pan. Add bacon, garlic and onion and cook 5 minutes over medium heat stirring regularly.

2 Add chilli and undrained, chopped tomatoes; reduce heat and simmer, uncovered, for 10 minutes.

3 Add cream and basil; cook for 1 minute.

4 Add sauce to pasta and toss well. Serve immediately.

COOK'S FILE

Storage time: This dish can be made up to the end of step 2, one day in advance.
Variation: Use a meat or pumpkin-filled pasta.

CHICKEN RAVIOLI WITH BUTTERED SAGE SAUCE

Preparation time: 15 minutes
Total cooking time: 10 minutes
Serves 4

500 g (1 lb 2 oz) fresh or dried
　chicken-filled ravioli or
　agnolotti
60 g (2¹/₄ oz) butter

4 spring onions (scallions),
　chopped
2 tablespoons fresh sage, chopped
50 g (¹/₂ cup) freshly grated
　Parmesan cheese, for serving
fresh sage leaves, extra, for
　garnish

➤ ADD RAVIOLI to a large pan of
rapidly boiling water.
1 Cook ravioli until just tender. Drain
pasta in colander and return to pan.

2 While ravioli is cooking, melt butter in a heavy-based pan. Add spring
onion and sage and stir for 2 minutes.
Add salt and pepper.
3 Add sauce to pasta; toss well. Pour
into a warmed serving platter and
sprinkle with Parmesan. Garnish with
fresh sage leaves; serve immediately.

COOK'S FILE

Hint: Bite through a piece of ravioli
to test whether it is done.

CHEESE TORTELLINI WITH NUTTY HERB SAUCE

Preparation time: 15 minutes
Total cooking time: 10 minutes
Serves 4–6

500 g (1 lb 2 oz) ham and cheese-
    filled fresh or dried tortellini
    or ravioli
100 g (3½ oz) walnuts

60 g (2¼ oz) butter
100 g (3½ oz) pine nuts
2 tablespoons chopped fresh
    parsley
2 teaspoons fresh thyme
60 g (¼ cup) fresh ricotta
    cheese
60 ml (¼ cup) cream

➤ ADD PASTA to a pan of rapidly boiling water and cook until just tender. Drain and return to pan.
1 Chop walnuts into small pieces.

While pasta is cooking, heat butter in heavy-based pan over medium heat until foaming.
2 Add walnuts and pine nuts and stir for 5 minutes or until golden brown. Add parsley, thyme, salt and pepper.
3 Beat ricotta with cream. Add Nutty Herb Sauce to pasta and toss well to combine. Top with a dollop of ricotta cream. Serve immediately.

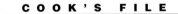

COOK'S FILE

Variation: Use chopped hazelnuts.

CANNELLONI

Preparation time: 35 minutes
Total cooking time: 1 hour 10 minutes
Serves 4–6

Beef and Spinach Filling
1 tablespoon olive oil
1 onion, chopped
1 garlic clove, crushed
500 g (1 lb 2 oz) minced
    (ground) beef
250 g (9 oz) packet frozen
    spinach, thawed
4 tablespoons tomato paste
    (purée)
125 g (¹/₂ cup) ricotta cheese
1 egg
¹/₂ teaspoon ground oregano

Bechamel Sauce
250 ml (1 cup) milk
1 sprig fresh parsley
5 peppercorns
30 g (1 oz) butter or margarine
1 tablespoon plain (all-purpose)
    flour
125 ml (¹/₂ cup) cream

Tomato Sauce
425 g (15 oz) can puréed
    tomato
2 tablespoons chopped fresh
    basil
1 garlic clove, crushed
¹/₂ teaspoon sugar

12–15 instant cannelloni tubes
150 g (1 cup) freshly grated
    mozzarella cheese
50 g (¹/₂ cup) freshly grated
    Parmesan cheese

► PREHEAT OVEN to 180°C (350°F/Gas 4). Lightly oil a large shallow casserole dish. Set aside.

1 To make Beef and Spinach Filling: Heat oil in a frying pan. Add onion and garlic and stir over low heat until onion is soft. Add beef and brown well, breaking up with a spoon or fork as it cooks. Add the spinach and tomato paste. Cook, stirring, for 1 minute. Remove from heat. In a small bowl, mix the ricotta, egg and oregano. Season to taste with salt and freshly ground black pepper. Add to beef mixture; stir to combine. Set aside.

2 To make Bechamel Sauce: Place milk, parsley and peppercorns in a small pan. Bring to the boil. Remove from heat. Allow to stand for 10 minutes. Strain, discard flavourings. Melt butter in a small pan. Add flour. Cook, stirring, for 1 minute. Remove from heat. Gradually blend in strained milk, stirring until mixture is smooth. Return to heat. Cook, stirring constantly over medium heat, until sauce boils and thickens. Reduce heat and simmer for 3 minutes. Add cream and season to taste, then stir.

3 To make Tomato Sauce: Place tomato purée, basil, garlic and sugar in a medium pan and stir to combine. Bring to the boil. Reduce heat. Simmer for 5 minutes.

4 Spoon the Beef and Spinach Filling into a piping bag and fill the cannelloni tubes or fill using a teaspoon.

5 Spoon a little of the Tomato Sauce in the base of the prepared casserole dish. Arrange cannelloni on top.

6 Pour the Bechamel Sauce over the cannelloni, followed by the remaining tomato sauce. Sprinkle combined cheeses over the top. Bake, uncovered, for 30–35 minutes, or until golden.

COOK'S FILE

Hint: Serve with a mixed green salad or steam some vegetables such as broccoli or beans, if desired.

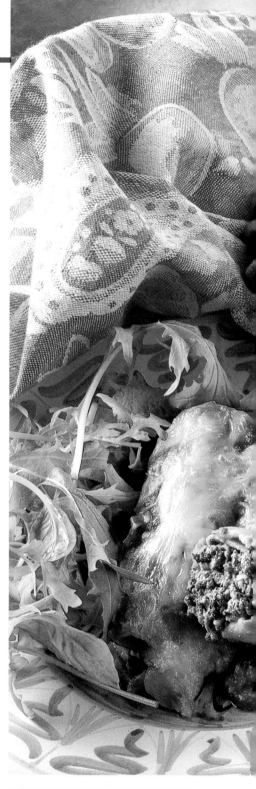

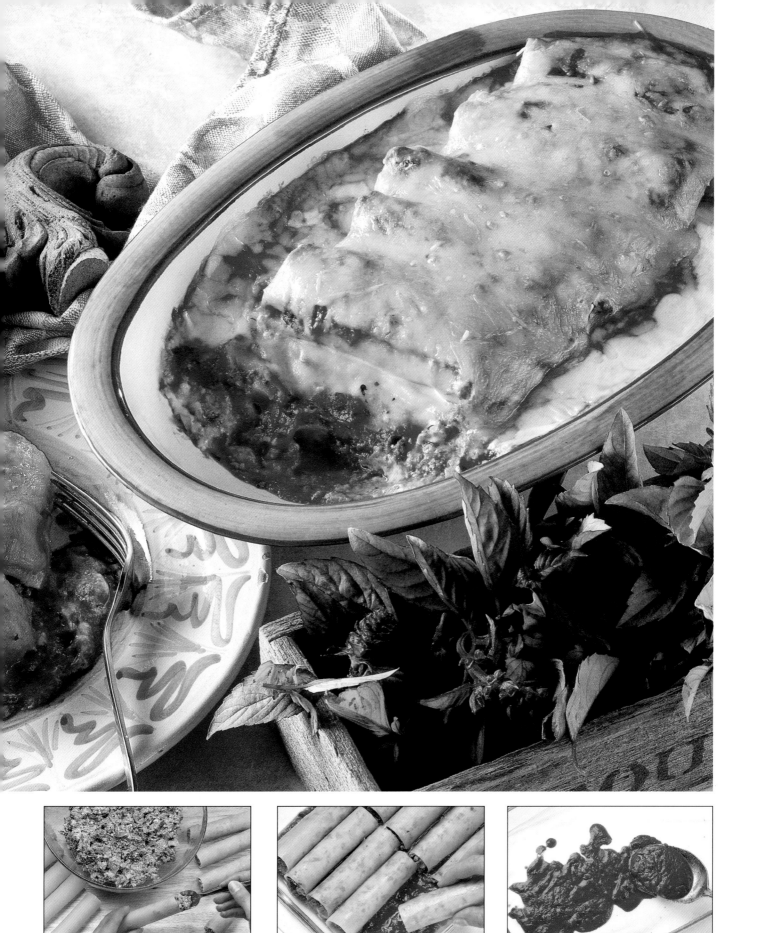

4

5

6

BAKED SPAGHETTI FRITTATA

Preparation time: 15 minutes
Total cooking time: 35 minutes
Serves 4

30 g (1 oz) butter or margarine
125 g (4¹/2 oz) mushrooms, sliced
1 capsicum (pepper), seeded and chopped
125 g (4¹/2 oz) ham, sliced

80 g (¹/2 cup) frozen peas
6 eggs
250 ml (1 cup) cream or milk
100 g (3¹/2 oz) spaghetti, cooked and chopped
2 tablespoons chopped fresh parsley
25 g (¹/4 cup) freshly grated Parmesan cheese

► PREHEAT OVEN to 180°C (350°F/Gas 4). Grease a 23 cm (9 inch) flan dish.
1 Melt butter in frying pan. Add mush-

rooms; cook over low heat 2–3 minutes.
2 Add capsicum; cook 1 minute. Stir in ham and peas. Remove pan from heat; allow mixture to cool slightly.
3 In a small bowl, whisk eggs and cream. Season to taste. Add spaghetti, parsley and mushroom mixture to bowl and stir. Pour into prepared dish and sprinkle with Parmesan cheese. Bake for 25–30 minutes.

COOK'S FILE

Hint: Serve with chargrilled vegetables and leafy salad greens.

1

2

3

BAKED SEAFOOD AND PASTA

Preparation time: 15 minutes
Total cooking time: 45 minutes
Serves 4–6

250 g (9 oz) packet instant lasagne sheets
500 g (1 lb 2 oz) boneless fish fillets
125 g (4 1/2 oz) scallops, cleaned
500 g (1 lb 2 oz) raw prawns (shrimp), shelled and deveined
125 g (4 1/2 oz) butter or margarine
1 leek, cleaned and sliced
85 g (2/3 cup) plain (all-purpose) flour
500 ml (2 cups) milk
500 ml (2 cups) dry white wine
125 g (1 cup) freshly grated Cheddar cheese

125 ml (1/2 cup) cream
25 g (1/2 cup) freshly grated Parmesan cheese
2 tablespoons chopped fresh parsley

➤ PREHEAT OVEN to 180°C (350°F/Gas 4). Line a greased shallow lasagne dish (about 24 x 30 cm/9 1/2 x 12 inch) with lasagne sheets, breaking them to fill any gaps. Set aside.

1 Chop fish and scallops into even-sized pieces. Chop prawns.

2 Melt the butter in large pan. Add the leek and cook, stirring, for 1 minute. Add the flour and cook, stirring, for 1 minute. Gradually blend in milk and wine, stirring until mixture is smooth. Cook, stirring constantly, over medium heat until sauce boils and thickens. Reduce heat and simmer for 3 minutes. Remove from heat; stir in cheese, salt and pepper. Add seafood; simmer for 1 minute. Remove from heat.

3 Spoon half the seafood mixture over lasagne sheets. Top with a layer of lasagne sheets. Continue layering, finishing with lasagne sheets.

4 Pour cream over the top. Sprinkle with combined parmesan and parsley. Bake, uncovered, for 30 minutes or until bubbling and golden.

COOK'S FILE

Note: Lasagne sheets are available in straight or ridged sheets.

MACARONI EGGPLANT CAKE

Preparation time: 30 minutes
Total cooking time: 1 hour
Serves 4–6

125 g (4¹/2 oz) macaroni
2–3 eggplant (aubergines),
 sliced thinly lengthwise
olive oil
1 onion, chopped
1 garlic clove, crushed
500 g (1 lb 2 oz) minced
 (ground) pork, beef or chicken
425 g (15 oz) can tomatoes
2 tablespoons tomato paste
 (purée)
80 g (¹/2 cup) frozen peas
150 g (1 cup) freshly grated
 mozzarella cheese
125 g (¹/2 cup) freshly grated
 Cheddar cheese

1 egg, beaten
50 g (¹/2 cup) freshly grated
 Parmesan cheese

➤ GREASE AND LINE a deep 23 cm (9 inch) round springform tin. Add macaroni to a large pan of rapidly boiling water and cook until just tender. Drain and set aside.

1 Arrange eggplant on trays. Sprinkle with salt. Allow to stand for 20 minutes. Rinse well. Pat dry with paper towels. Heat 2 tablespoons oil in a frying pan. Cook eggplant in batches in a single layer until golden on each side. Add more oil as required. Drain on paper towels.

2 Add onion and crushed garlic to same pan and stir over low heat until onion is tender. Add meat and brown, breaking up any lumps with a spoon or fork as it cooks. Add undrained, crushed tomatoes and tomato paste. Season with salt and

freshly ground black pepper and stir well. Bring to the boil, then reduce the heat and simmer for 15–20 minutes. Set aside.

3 In a bowl, place peas, macaroni, mozzarella and Cheddar cheeses, egg and half the Parmesan. Use a wooden spoon to mix. Set aside.

4 Preheat oven to 180°C (350°F/Gas

4). Place a slice of eggplant in the centre on the base of prepared tin. Arrange three-quarters of remaining eggplant in an overlapping pattern to completely cover the base and sides of tin. Sprinkle with half the remaining parmesan cheese.

5 Combine the meat mixture with macaroni mixture. Carefully spoon filling into eggplant case, packing down well. Arrange remaining eggplant slices, overlapping, over the filling. Sprinkle with the remaining parmesan cheese.

6 Bake, uncovered, 25–30 minutes or until golden. Allow to rest for 5 minutes before unmoulding onto a serving plate. Serve with salad, if desired.

COOK'S FILE

Variations: If preferred, omit the minced meat and add chopped cooked Italian sausage and chopped cooked chicken to the tomato mixture.

Serve with some extra tomato sauce made by simmering undrained, crushed tomatoes with a little garlic, pepper and chopped basil until thickened.

CONCHIGLIE WITH CHICKEN AND RICOTTA

Preparation time: 15 minutes
Total cooking time: 1 hour 10 minutes
Serves 4

500 g (1 lb 2 oz) conchiglie
   (shell pasta)
2 tablespoons olive oil
1 onion, chopped
1 garlic clove, crushed
60 g (2¼ oz) prosciutto, sliced
125 g (4½ oz) mushrooms,
   chopped
250 g (9 oz) minced (ground)
   chicken
2 tablespoons tomato paste
   (purée)
425 g (15 oz) can tomatoes
125 ml (½ cup) dry white wine
1 teaspoon dried oregano

250 g (9 oz) ricotta cheese
150 g (1 cup) grated mozzarella
1 teaspoon snipped fresh chives
1 tablespoon chopped parsley
25 g (¼ cup) freshly grated
   Parmesan cheese

➤ ADD CONCHIGLIE TO a large pan of rapidly boiling water and cook until just tender. Drain well.

1 Heat oil in a large frying pan. Add onion and garlic and stir over low heat until onion is tender. Add prosciutto and stir for 1 minute.

2 Add mushrooms to pan and cook for 2 minutes. Add meat. Brown well, breaking up lumps with a fork.

3 Stir in tomato paste, undrained crushed tomatoes, wine, oregano, salt and pepper. Bring to the boil. Reduce heat. Simmer for 20 minutes.

4 Preheat oven to 180°C (350°F/Gas 4). Combine ricotta, mozzarella, chives,

parsley and half the Parmesan. Spoon a little of the mixture into each shell. Spoon some of the chicken sauce into the base of a casserole dish. Arrange shells on top. Spread remaining sauce over the top. Sprinkle with remaining Parmesan. Bake 25–30 minutes, or until golden.

COOK'S FILE

Note: Shell pastas vary in size—medium or large shells are best for this dish.

VEAL TORTELLINI WITH CREAMY SPINACH SAUCE

Preparation time: 15 minutes
Total cooking time: 20 minutes
Serves 4

500 g (1 lb 2 oz) fresh or dried
    veal-filled tortellini
350 g (12 oz) frozen spinach
60 g (2^1/$_4$ oz) butter
1 onion, chopped
1 garlic clove, crushed

^{1}/$_2$ teaspoon nutmeg
300 ml (1^1/$_4$ cups) cream
125 ml (^{1}/$_2$ cup) light chicken
    stock
25 g (^{1}/$_4$ cup) grated pecorino
    cheese, for serving

➤ ADD PASTA to a large pan of rapidly boiling water.

1 Cook pasta until just tender. Drain and return to pan. While pasta is cooking, allow spinach to thaw.

2 Melt butter in a heavy-based pan. Add the onion and garlic; cook over low heat, stirring regularly, for 5 minutes or until golden.

3 Add drained spinach, nutmeg, cream and stock to pan. Bring to boil and simmer for 3 minutes. Season with salt and freshly ground black pepper. Add the sauce to the pasta and toss to combine. Serve in warmed pasta bowls. Sprinkle with pecorino cheese and serve immediately.

COOK'S FILE

Note: You can use fresh spinach—chop leaves; steam and add to sauce.

1

2

3

TORTELLINI WITH MUSHROOM SAUCE

Preparation time: 25 minutes
Total cooking time: 1 hour 30 minutes
Serves 4

Pasta
250 g (2 cups) plain (all-purpose) flour
pinch salt
3 eggs
1 tablespoon olive oil

Filling
125 g (4^1/2 oz) packet frozen spinach, thawed, excess liquid removed
125 g (4^1/2 oz) tub ricotta cheese
2 tablespoons freshly grated Parmesan cheese
1 egg, beaten

Sauce
1 tablespoon olive oil
1 garlic clove, crushed
125 g (4^1/2 oz) mushrooms, sliced
250 ml (1 cup) cream
25 g (^{1}/4 cup) freshly grated Parmesan cheese

➤ **TO MAKE PASTA:** Sift flour and salt onto a board. Make a well in the centre of the flour.

1 In a jug, whisk together the eggs, oil and 1 tablespoon water. Add the egg mixture gradually to the flour, working in with your hands until the mixture forms a ball. Add a little extra water if necessary. Knead on a lightly floured surface for 5 minutes, or until the dough is smooth and elastic. Place the dough in a lightly oiled bowl. Cover with plastic wrap and allow to stand for 30 minutes.

2 To make Filling: In a bowl, combine the drained spinach, ricotta and Parmesan cheeses and beaten egg. Season to taste with salt and freshly ground black pepper. Set aside.

3 To make Sauce: Heat the oil in a frying pan. Add the garlic and stir over low heat for 30 seconds. Add the mushrooms and cook for 3 minutes. Pour in the cream. Set aside.

4 Roll the dough on a lightly floured surface until about 1 mm (^{1}/16 inch) thick. Using a floured cutter, cut into 5 cm (2 inch) rounds. Spoon about ^{1}/2 teaspoon of Filling in the centre of each round. Brush a little water around the edge of each round. Fold rounds in half to form a semi-circle. Press edges together firmly. Wrap each semi-circle around your forefinger to form a ring. Press ends of dough together firmly.

5 Cook the tortellini in batches in a large saucepan of rapidly boiling water for about 8 minutes each batch—until just tender. Drain well, then return to the pan. Keep warm.

6 Return Sauce to medium heat. Bring to the boil. Reduce the heat and simmer for 3 minutes. Add the Parmesan cheese and season with salt and freshly ground black pepper; stir well. Add the Sauce to the tortellini and toss until well combined. Divide the tortellini and sauce among individual warmed serving bowls.

COOK'S FILE

Hints: Serve sprinkled with some freshly grated Parmesan cheese and chopped fresh parsley.

Steamed vegetables such as sliced carrots, pumpkin and zucchini (courgette) can be served separately. Or, serve with your choice of salad.

Note: Freshly made tortellini and ravioli pastas are worth the extra care and time—the results are delicious.

1

2

3

4

5

6

MACARONI CHEESE

Preparation time: 15 minutes
Total cooking time: 35 minutes
Serves 4

500 ml (2 cups) milk
250 ml (1 cup) cream
1 bay leaf
1 whole clove
1/2 cinnamon stick
60 g (2 1/4 oz) butter or margarine
2 tablespoons plain (all-purpose)
   flour
250 g (2 cups) freshly grated
   Cheddar cheese
50 g (1/2 cup) freshly grated
   Parmesan cheese

375 g (13 oz) elbow macaroni
80 g (1 cup) fresh breadcrumbs
2 rashers rindless bacon,
   chopped and fried until crisp

➤ PREHEAT OVEN to 180°C
(350°F/Gas 4).
1 Place milk and cream in a medium
saucepan with bay leaf, clove and cinnamon stick. Bring to the boil.
Remove from heat. Allow to stand for
10 minutes. Strain into a jug; remove
and discard flavourings.
2 Melt butter in a saucepan. Add
flour and stir over low heat for
1 minute. Remove from heat.
Gradually add milk and cream mixture, stirring until smooth. Return to
heat. Cook, stirring constantly, until

sauce boils and thickens. Reduce heat;
simmer 3 minutes. Remove from heat
and add 125 g (1 cup) of the Cheddar
cheese, 25 g (1/4 cup) of the Parmesan.
Season to taste with salt and freshly
ground black pepper. Set aside.
3 Add macaroni to a large pan of
rapidly boiling water and cook until
just tender. Drain well and return to
the pan. Add sauce and mix well.
Spoon into a deep casserole dish.
Sprinkle with combined breadcrumbs,
bacon and remaining cheeses. Bake
for 15–20 minutes, or until golden.

COOK'S FILE

Variation: You can add chopped
cooked chicken to the white sauce
before mixing with the pasta.

PASTITSIO

Preparation time: 20 minutes
Total cooking time: 1 hour
Serves 4–6

250 g (9 oz) tubular spaghetti
250 g (9 oz) tub ricotta cheese
60 g (2¹/₄ oz) prosciutto, chopped
1 egg, beaten
1 tablespoon freshly grated Parmesan cheese
¹/₄ teaspoon ground nutmeg

Meat Sauce
2 tablespoons olive oil
1 onion, chopped
1 garlic clove, crushed
500 g (1 lb 2 oz) minced (ground) beef
425 g (15 oz) can tomatoes
125 ml (¹/₂ cup) red wine
125 ml (¹/₂ cup) beef stock
2 tablespoons tomato paste (purée)
2 tablespoons chopped fresh parsley
¹/₂ teaspoon ground oregano

Cheese Sauce
60 g (2¹/₄ oz) butter or margarine
30 g (¹/₄ cup) plain (all-purpose) flour
375 ml (1¹/₂ cups) milk
250 ml (1 cup) cream
2 eggs, beaten
125 g (1 cup) freshly grated Cheddar cheese
¹/₄ teaspoon ground nutmeg
20 g (¹/₄ cup) fresh breadcrumbs
25 g (¹/₄ cup) freshly grated Parmesan cheese

➤ PREHEAT OVEN to 180°C (350°F/

Gas 4). Oil a 28 x 20 cm (11 x 8 inch) ovenproof dish.

1 Cook pasta in large pan of rapidly boiling water until just tender; drain well. Allow to cool slightly; return to pan. Add ricotta, prosciutto, egg, parmesan, nutmeg, salt and pepper to pasta. Press into prepared dish. Set aside.

2 To make Meat Sauce: Heat oil in large pan. Add onion and garlic; stir over low heat until onion is tender. Add meat; brown well, breaking up lumps with a fork. Add undrained crushed tomatoes, wine, stock, tomato paste, parsley, oregano, salt and pepper; stir. Bring to the boil. Reduce heat. Simmer, uncovered, for 20 minutes.

Spoon over the pasta layer. Set aside.

3 To make Cheese Sauce: Melt butter in medium pan. Add flour and cook, stirring, for 1 minute. Remove from heat. Gradually add milk and cream, stirring until smooth. Return to heat. Cook, stirring constantly, until sauce boils and thickens. Reduce heat; simmer 3 minutes. Remove from heat. Whisk in eggs, cheese, nutmeg, salt and pepper. Spoon over meat layer. Sprinkle with combined breadcrumbs and Parmesan. Bake 20–25 minutes.

COOK'S FILE

Storage time: Meat sauce can be made a day ahead and refrigerated.

1

2

3

RAVIOLI

Preparation time: 45 minutes +
 30 minutes standing
Total cooking time: 2 hours 45 minutes
Serves 4

Pasta
250 g (2 cups) plain (all-purpose)
 flour
pinch salt
3 eggs
1 tablespoon olive oil
1 egg yolk, extra

Filling
125 g (4¹/₂ oz) minced (ground)
 chicken
75 g (2¹/₂ oz) ricotta or cottage
 cheese
60 g (2¹/₄ oz) chicken livers,
 trimmed and chopped
30 g (1 oz) prosciutto, chopped
1 slice salami, chopped
2 tablespoons freshly grated
 Parmesan cheese
1 egg, beaten
1 tablespoon chopped fresh
 parsley
1 garlic clove, crushed
¹/₄ teaspoon mixed spice

Tomato Sauce
2 tablespoons olive oil
1 onion, finely chopped
2 garlic cloves, crushed
2 x 425 g (15 oz) cans tomatoes
15 g (¹/₄ cup) chopped fresh
 basil
¹/₂ teaspoon mixed herbs

➤ **TO MAKE PASTA:** Sift flour
and salt onto a board. Make a well in
the centre of the flour.

1 In a bowl, whisk together the eggs,
oil and 1 tablespoon water. Add the
egg mixture gradually to the flour,
working in with hand until mixture
forms a ball. Knead on a lightly
floured surface for 5 minutes, or until
smooth and elastic. Place dough in a
lightly oiled bowl. Cover with plastic
wrap. Allow to stand for 30 minutes.

2 To make Filling: Place the ingredients in a food processor. Process
until finely chopped. Set aside.

3 To make Tomato Sauce: Heat
the oil in a pan. Add the onion and
garlic and stir over low heat until
onion softens. Increase heat, add
undrained, crushed tomatoes, basil
and mixed herbs. Season with salt and
ground black pepper, then stir. Bring
to the boil. Reduce heat and simmer
for 15 minutes. Remove from heat.

4 Roll out half the dough until 1 mm
(¹/₁₆ inch) thick. Cut with a knife or
fluted pastry cutter into 10 cm (4 inch)
strips. Place teaspoons of filling at
5 cm (2 inch) intervals down one side
of each strip. Whisk together extra
egg yolk and 60 ml (¹/₄ cup) water.
Brush along one side of dough and
between filling. Fold dough over filling to meet the other side. Repeat with
remaining filling and dough.

5 Press edges of dough together firmly to seal. Cut between the mounds of
filling with a knife or a fluted pastry
cutter.

6 Cook ravioli in batches in a large
pan of rapidly boiling water for
10 minutes each batch. Reheat
Tomato Sauce in a large pan. Add
cooked ravioli and toss well until
sauce is evenly distributed. Simmer,
stirring, for 5 minutes. Garnish with
sprigs of fresh herbs, if desired.

COOK'S FILE

Hint: Serve with crusty bread and a
light salad.
Note: If preferred, pasta dough may
be made with only 2 eggs— however, it
will require extra kneading.

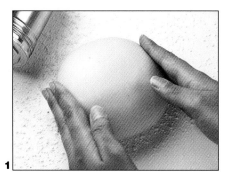

1

2

3

4

5

6

BAKED CANNELLONI MILANESE

Preparation time: 20 minutes
Total cooking time: 1 hour 50 minutes
Serves 4

500 g (1 lb 2 oz) minced (ground)
   pork and veal
50 g (¹/₂ cup) dry breadcrumbs
50 g (¹/₂ cup) freshly grated
   Parmesan cheese
2 eggs, beaten
1 teaspoon dried oregano
12–15 cannelloni tubes
375 g (13 oz) fresh ricotta
   cheese
50 g (¹/₂ cup) freshly grated
   Parmesan cheese
60 g (¹/₂ cup) freshly grated
   Cheddar cheese

Tomato Sauce
425 g (15 oz) can puréed tomato
425 g (15 oz) can tomatoes
2 garlic cloves, crushed
15 g (¹/₄ cup) chopped fresh
   basil

➤ PREHEAT OVEN to 180°C
(350°F/Gas 4). Lightly grease a rectangular casserole dish.

1 In a medium bowl, combine meat, breadcrumbs, Parmesan cheese, beaten egg and oregano. Season with salt and black pepper. Use a teaspoon to stuff the cannelloni tubes with meat mixture. Set aside.

2 To make Tomato Sauce: Place puréed tomato, undrained crushed tomatoes and garlic in medium pan. Bring to the boil. Reduce heat. Simmer for 15 minutes. Add basil and season with pepper and stir well.

3 Spoon half the Tomato Sauce over the base of prepared dish.

4 Arrange the stuffed cannelloni tubes on top. Cover with remaining sauce. Spread with ricotta cheese. Sprinkle with combined Parmesan and Cheddar cheeses. Bake, covered with foil, for 1 hour. Uncover and bake for another 15 minutes, or until golden. Cut into squares for serving.

COOK'S FILE

Hint: Serve with tomato quarters and mixed green salad. Garnish with sprigs of fresh herbs.

BAKED FETTUCCINE

Preparation time: 20 minutes
Total cooking time: 25 minutes
Serves 4

500 g (1 lb 2 oz) spinach
    fettuccine
60 g (2$^{1}/_{4}$ oz) butter or
    margarine
1 onion, finely chopped
300 ml (10$^{1}/_{2}$ fl oz) sour cream
250 ml (1 cup) cream

$^{1}/_{4}$ teaspoon ground nutmeg
50 g ($^{1}/_{2}$ cup) freshly grated
    Parmesan cheese
150 g (1 cup) freshly grated
    mozzarella cheese

➤ PREHEAT OVEN to 180°C
(350°F/Gas 4).
1 Add fettuccine to a large pan of
rapidly boiling water and cook until
just tender. Drain well and set aside.
Meanwhile, melt butter in a large pan.
Add onion and stir over low heat until
onion softens. Add fettuccine to pan.

2 Add sour cream to the pan and
toss well. Simmer, stirring, until pasta
is well coated.
3 Add the cream, ground nutmeg
and 25 g ($^{1}/_{4}$ cup) of the Parmesan.
Season with salt and ground black
pepper and stir. Pour into a greased
casserole dish. Sprinkle with combined mozzarella and remaining
Parmesan. Bake for 15 minutes, or
until cheese is softened and golden.

COOK'S FILE

Hint: Serve with a mixed salad.

CLASSIC LASAGNE

Preparation time: 25 minutes
Total cooking time: 1 hour 15 minutes
Serves 4–6

250 g (9 oz) packet instant
  lasagne sheets
75 g (^{1}/2 cup) freshly grated
  mozzarella cheese
60 g (^{1}/2 cup) freshly grated
  Cheddar cheese
125 ml (^{1}/2 cup) cream
25 g (^{1}/4 cup) freshly grated
  Parmesan cheese

Cheese Sauce
60 g (2^1/4 oz) butter or margarine
40 g (^{1}/3 cup) plain (all-purpose)
  flour
500 ml (2 cups) milk
120 g (1 cup) freshly grated
  Cheddar cheese

Meat Sauce
1 tablespoon olive oil
1 onion, finely chopped
1 garlic clove, crushed
500 g (1 lb 2 oz) minced (ground)
  beef
2 x 425 g (15 oz) cans tomatoes
60 ml (^{1}/4 cup) red wine
^{1}/2 teaspoon ground oregano
^{1}/4 teaspoon ground basil

➤ PREHEAT OVEN to 180°C
(350°F/Gas 4).
1 Brush a shallow oblong ovenproof
dish (about 24 x 30 cm/9^1/2 x 12 inch)
with melted butter or oil. Line with
lasagne sheets, breaking them to fill
any gaps. Set aside.
2 To make Cheese Sauce: Melt
butter in a medium saucepan. Add the
flour and stir for 1 minute. Remove
from heat. Gradually add the milk,
stirring until the mixture is smooth.
Return to the heat. Cook, stirring

constantly, over medium heat until the
sauce boils and thickens. Reduce heat
and simmer for 3 minutes. Remove
from heat, add cheese and season to
taste with salt and freshly ground
black pepper; stir until well combined.
Set aside.
3 To make Meat Sauce: Heat the
oil in a large pan. Add the onion and
garlic and stir over low heat until
onion softens. Add the meat. Brown

well, breaking up with a fork as it cooks. Stir in undrained, crushed tomatoes, wine, oregano and basil. Season with salt and freshly ground black pepper. Bring to boil. Reduce heat; simmer 20 minutes.

4 Spoon one-third of the meat sauce over lasagne sheets. Top with one-third of the cheese sauce. Arrange layer of lasagne sheets over top.

5 Continue layering, finishing with lasagne sheets. Sprinkle with combined mozzarella and Cheddar cheese.

6 Pour cream over the top. Sprinkle with Parmesan. Bake for 35–40 minutes, or until bubbling and golden.

COOK'S FILE

Note: Cheese sauce is a variation of Bechamel Sauce. A true Bechamel uses milk infused with flavourings such as bay leaf, cloves, peppercorns, parsley sprig and cinnamon stick. To do this, bring milk to boiling point (without boiling—known as scalding) with one or more of the flavourings and allow to stand for 10 minutes before straining. To prevent sauce forming a skin, cover surface completely with plastic wrap or greased greaseproof paper until required.

Sauces are easier to handle if allowed to cool before layering.

PASTA AND SPINACH TIMBALE

Preparation time: 15 minutes
Total cooking time: 35 minutes
Serves 6

30 g (1 oz) butter or
   margarine
1 tablespoon olive oil
1 onion, chopped
1 bunch cooked, well-drained
   spinach
8 eggs, beaten
250 ml (1 cup) cream
100 g (3¹/₂ oz) spaghetti or
   tagliolini, cooked

60 g (¹/₂ cup) freshly grated
   Cheddar cheese
50 g (¹/₂ cup) freshly grated
   Parmesan cheese

➤ PREHEAT OVEN to 180°C (350°F/Gas 4). Brush six 250 ml (1 cup) capacity moulds with melted butter or oil. Line bases with baking paper.

1 Heat butter and oil together in a frying pan. Add onion and stir over low heat until onion softens. Add well-drained spinach and cook for 1 minute. Remove from heat and allow to cool. Whisk in eggs and cream. Stir in the spaghetti or tagliolini and grated cheeses. Season to taste with salt and freshly ground black pepper and stir well. Spoon into prepared moulds.

2 Place moulds in a baking dish. Pour boiling water into baking dish to come halfway up sides of moulds. Bake for 30–35 minutes or until set. Halfway through cooking, you may need to cover top with a sheet of foil to prevent excess browning. Near the end of cooking time, test timbales with the point of a knife. When cooked, the knife should come out clean.

3 Allow timbales to rest 15 minutes. Run point of a knife around edge of each mould. Invert onto serving plates.

COOK'S FILE

Hints: Serve with a tomato sauce.

1

2

3

PASTA PIE

Preparation time: 15 minutes
Total cooking time: 55 minutes
Serves 4

250 g (9 oz) macaroni
1 tablespoon olive oil
1 onion, sliced
125 g (4¹/2 oz) pancetta,
   chopped
125 g (4¹/2 oz) ham, chopped
4 eggs
250 ml (1 cup) milk
250 ml (1 cup) cream

2 tablespoons snipped fresh
   chives
120 g (1 cup) freshly grated
   Cheddar cheese
125 g (4¹/2 oz) bocconcini
   (about 4), chopped

➤ PREHEAT OVEN to 180°C
(350°F/Gas 4).

1 Add the macaroni to a large pan of rapidly boiling water and cook until just tender. Drain thoroughly. Spread evenly over the base of a 5 cm (2 inch) deep casserole dish.

2 Heat the oil in a large frying pan. Add the sliced onion and stir over low heat until tender. Add the chopped pancetta to pan and cook for 2 minutes. Add ham to the mixture and stir well. Remove from the heat and allow to cool.

3 In a bowl, whisk together eggs, milk, cream and chives. Season with salt and freshly ground black pepper. Add Cheddar cheese, chopped bocconcini and the pancetta mixture and stir well. Spread evenly over top of macaroni. Bake for 35–40 minutes, or until mixture is set.

COOK'S FILE

Hint: Serve with slices of egg tomato.

1

2

3

TORTELLINI WITH MUSHROOM AND GRUYERE SAUCE

Preparation time: 15 minutes
Total cooking time: 25 minutes
Serves 4–6

500 g (1 lb 2 oz) fresh or dried chicken- or veal-filled herb tortellini
100 g (3½ oz) butter
3 spring onions (scallions), chopped

200 g (7 oz) baby mushrooms, sliced
2 tablespoons plain (all-purpose) flour
375 ml (1½ cups) milk
125 ml (½ cup) cream
100 g (3½ oz) freshly grated Gruyère cheese
80 g (½ cup) pine nuts, toasted

➤ BRING A LARGE PAN of water to the boil.

1 Add tortellini and cook until just tender. Drain and keep warm.

2 Melt half the butter in medium pan, add spring onion and sliced mushrooms. Cook over medium heat for 3 minutes, or until softened. Set aside.

3 In another pan, melt remaining butter. Add flour stir over low heat for 2 minutes. Gradually add milk and cream, stirring constantly until sauce boils and thickens. Add the cheese and season to taste with salt and freshly ground black pepper; stir well. Combine with mushrooms. Arrange the tortellini in a serving bowl, then pour the sauce over. Sprinkle with pine nuts and extra chopped spring onion, if desired.

PASTA-FILLED VEGETABLES

Preparation time: 20 minutes
Total cooking time: 45 minutes
Serves 4–6

1 tablespoon olive oil
1 onion, finely chopped
1 garlic clove, crushed
3 rashers rindless bacon, finely
    chopped
150 g (5½ oz) risoni, cooked
150 g (1 cup) freshly grated
    mozzarella cheese
50 g (½ cup) freshly grated
    Parmesan cheese
2 tablespoons chopped fresh
    parsley
4 large red capsicum (peppers),
    halved lengthwise, seeds
    removed
425 g (15 oz) can tomatoes
125 ml (½ cup) dry white wine
1 tablespoon tomato paste
    (purée)
½ teaspoon ground oregano
2 tablespoons chopped fresh basil

➤ PREHEAT OVEN to 180°C (350°F/Gas 4). Lightly oil a large shallow ovenproof dish.

1 Heat oil in a pan. Add onion and garlic and stir over low heat until onion softens. Add bacon; stir until crisp.

2 Transfer bacon mixture to large bowl and combine with risoni, cheeses and parsley. Spoon mixture into capsicum halves. Arrange in dish.

3 In bowl, combine undrained, crushed tomatoes, wine, tomato paste and oregano. Season. Spoon over risoni mixture. Sprinkle with basil. Bake for 35–40 minutes.

COOK'S FILE

Hint: Serve with baked chicken.

PASTA SOUFFLE

Preparation time: 20 minutes
Total cooking time: 55 minutes
Serves 4

2 tablespoons freshly grated
  Parmesan cheese
60 g (2¼ oz) butter or
  margarine
1 small onion, finely chopped
2 tablespoons plain (all-purpose)
  flour
500 ml (2 cups) milk
125 ml (½ cup) chicken stock
3 eggs, separated
125 g (4½ oz) small macaroni,
  cooked
210 g (7¼ oz) can salmon,
  drained and flaked
1 tablespoon chopped fresh
  parsley
zest of 1 lemon

➤ PREHEAT OVEN to 210°C
(415°F/Gas 6–7).
1 Brush a round 6-cup (18 cm/7 inch)
soufflé dish with oil. Coat base and
sides with Parmesan. Shake off excess.
To Collar a Soufflé Dish: Cut a
piece of aluminium foil or greaseproof
paper 5 cm (2 inch) longer than the
circumference of the dish. Fold in half
lengthways. Wrap foil around the outside of the dish, extending 5 cm (2 inch)
above the rim. Secure with string.
2 Heat butter in a large pan. Add
onion and cook over low heat until
tender. Add flour. Stir 2 minutes, or
until mixture is lightly golden.
Remove from heat. Gradually blend in
milk and stock, stirring until mixture
is smooth. Return to heat. Stir constantly over medium heat until mixture boils and thickens. Reduce heat
and simmer for 3 minutes. Add egg
yolks and whisk until smooth. Add

macaroni, salmon, parsley and lemon
zest. Season. Stir until combined.
Transfer mixture to a large bowl.
3 Using electric beaters, beat egg
whites in a small dry mixing bowl
until stiff peaks form. Using a metal
spoon, fold gently into salmon mixture. Spoon into prepared dish. Bake
for 40–45 minutes or until well risen
and browned. Serve immediately.

COOK'S FILE

Storage time: Hot soufflés should be
made just before you want to serve
them as they will collapse very quickly after removal from the oven. The
base mixture can be prepared, up to
the end of Step 2, well in advance.
Soften the mixture before folding in
beaten egg whites. Whites should be
folded into mixture just before cooking.

1

2

3

BAKED MEATBALLS AND PASTA

Preparation time: 25 minutes
Total cooking time: 55 minutes
Serves 4

100 g (3¹/2 oz) macaroni
500 g (1 lb 2 oz) minced
   (ground) beef
1 onion, finely chopped
40 g (¹/2 cup) fresh breadcrumbs
2 tablespoons freshly grated
   Parmesan cheese
1 tablespoon chopped fresh basil
1 egg, beaten
2 tablespoons olive oil
1 cup freshly grated mozzarella
   cheese
40 g (¹/2 cup) fresh breadcrumbs

Sauce
1 onion, sliced

1 garlic clove, crushed
1 capsicum (pepper), seeded
   and sliced
125 g (4¹/2 oz) mushrooms, sliced
4 tablespoons tomato paste
   (purée)
125 ml (¹/2 cup) red wine

➤ ADD MACARONI TO a large pan of rapidly boiling water and cook until just tender. Drain, set aside.
1 In a bowl, combine meat, onion, breadcrumbs, Parmesan, basil and egg. Form heaped teaspoonsful into small balls.
2 Heat oil in a frying pan. Add meatballs and cook until well browned. Drain on paper towels. Transfer to an ovenproof dish. Preheat oven to 180°C (350°F/Gas 4).
3 To make Sauce: Add onion and garlic to same pan; stir over low heat until onion is tender. Add capsicum and mushrooms; cook 2 minutes. Stir

4

in tomato paste. Combine wine and 250 ml (1 cup) water; add to pan. Bring to boil, stirring. Mix in macaroni and season. Pour over top of meatballs.
4 Bake, uncovered, for 30–35 minutes. Sprinkle with combined mozzarella cheese and breadcrumbs. Bake for another 10 minutes, or until golden.

COOK'S FILE

Note: Macaroni comes in many differing shapes and sizes—choose whichever you prefer.

SEMOLINA GNOCCHI

Preparation time: 15 minutes +
  1 hour refrigeration
Total cooking time: 40 minutes
Serves 4

750 ml (3 cups) milk
$^1/_4$ teaspoon ground nutmeg
85 g ($^2/_3$ cup) semolina
1 egg, beaten
150 g ($1^1/_2$ cups) freshly grated
  Parmesan cheese
60 g ($2^1/_4$ oz) butter or
  margarine, melted

125 ml ($^1/_2$ cup) cream
75 g ($^1/_2$ cup) freshly grated
  mozzarella cheese
$^1/_4$ teaspoon ground nutmeg, extra

► LINE A DEEP 29 x 19 x 3 cm
($11^1/_2$ x $7^1/_2$ x $1^1/_4$ inch) swiss roll tin
with baking paper.
1 Place milk and nutmeg in a medium pan. Season with salt and pepper.
Bring to the boil. Reduce heat and
gradually stir in semolina. Cook, stirring occasionally, for 5–10 minutes, or
until semolina is very stiff. Remove
from heat. Add egg and 100 g (1 cup)
Parmesan cheese to semolina mixture

and stir to combine. Spread mixture in
prepared tin. Refrigerate for 1 hour, or
until firm.
2 Preheat the oven to 180°C
(350°F/Gas 4). Cut semolina into
rounds using a floured 4 cm ($1^1/_2$ inch)
cutter. Arrange in a greased shallow
casserole dish.
3 Pour butter over top, followed by
cream. Sprinkle with combined
remaining Parmesan and mozzarella
cheese. Sprinkle with extra nutmeg.
Bake 20–25 minutes, or until golden.

COOK'S FILE

Hint: Serve with mixed salad.

1

2

3

INDEX

USEFUL INFORMATION

All our recipes are tested in a special test kitchen. Standard metric measuring cups and spoons are used in the development of our recipes. All cup and spoon measurements are level. We have used 60 g (2¼ oz/Grade 3) eggs in all recipes. Sizes of cans vary from manufacturer to manufacturer and between countries—use the can size closest to the one suggested in the recipe.

Conversion Guide

1 cup	= 250 ml (9 fl oz)
1 teaspoon	= 5 ml
1 Australian tablespoon	= 20 ml (4 teaspoons)
1 UK/US tablespoon	= 15 ml (3 teaspoons)

NOTE: We have used 20 ml tablespoon measures. If you are using a 15 ml tablespoon, for most recipes the difference will not be noticeable. However, for recipes using baking powder, gelatine, bicarbonate of soda, small amounts of flour and cornflour, add an extra teaspoon for each tablespoon specified.

Oven Temperatures

Cooking times may vary slightly depending on the type of oven you are using. Before you preheat the oven, we suggest that you refer to the manufacturer's instructions to ensure proper temperature control.

	°C	°F	Gas Mark
Very slow	120	250	½
Slow	150	300	2
Warm	170	325	3
Moderate	180	350	4
Mod. hot	190	375	5
Mod. hot	200	400	6
Hot	220	425	7
Very hot	230	450	8

NOTE: For fan-forced ovens check your appliance manual, but as a general rule, set oven temperature to 20°C lower than the temperature indicated in the recipe.

Dry Measures
30 g	= 1 oz
250 g	= 9 oz
500 g	= 1 lb 2 oz

Liquid Measures
30 ml	= 1 fl oz
125 ml	= 4 fl oz
250 ml	= 9 fl oz

Linear Measures
6 mm	= ¼ inch
1 cm	= ½ inch
2.5 cm	= 1 inch

Cup Conversions

1 cup plain (all-purpose) flour	= 125 g (4½ oz)
1 cup grated Parmesan cheese	= 100 g (3½ oz)
1 cup grated mozzarella cheese	= 150 g (5½ oz)
1 cup grated Cheddar cheese	= 125 g (4½ oz)
1 cup fresh breadcrumbs	= 80 g (3 oz)
1 cup peas	= 155 g (5½ oz)
1 cup chopped parsley	= 60 g (2¼ oz)
1 cup black olives (unpitted)	= 175 g (6 oz)
1 cup tomato paste	= 250 g (9 oz)

International Glossary

broad beans	lima beans
capsicum	red or green pepper
chilli	chili pepper, chile
eggplant	aubergine
plain flour	all-purpose flour
red onion	Spanish onion
silverbeet	Swiss chard

This edition published in 2003 by Bay Books, an imprint of Murdoch Magazines Pty Limited, GPO Box 1203, Sydney NSW 2001, Australia.

Managing Editor: Rachel Carter.
Editor: Wendy Stephen.
Food Director: Jane Lawson.
Food Editors: Kerrie Ray, Tracy Rutherford.
Designer: Marylouise Brammer.
Recipe Development: Jo Richardson, Jennene Plummer, Janelle Bloom.
Home Economists: Wendy Brodhurst, Wendy Goggin, Angela Nahas, Maria Sampsonis, Michelle Lawton, Jo Forrest.
Photographers: Luis Martin, Reg Morrison (Steps).
Food Stylist: Mary Harris.
Food Stylist's Assistant: Christine Sheppard.

Chief Executive: Juliet Rogers. **Publisher:** Kay Scarlett.

ISBN 0 86411 414 1.
Printed by Sing Cheong Printing Co. Ltd. PRINTED IN CHINA.